This book is dedicated to
my mother and my father.

ACKNOWLEDGMENTS

Many people have, in different ways, enabled me to write this book. I owe many thanks to Carol Martin, Georgia Lepper, James Smith, and particularly to Christopher Bollas for helpful comments on an earlier manuscript. Many thanks also to the late Lionel Monteith, founder of the Lincoln Clinic, and to Patricia Braybrooks, who started me off on this road, and to Ralph Layland for his interest in seeing this book completed. I would also like to thank Sharon Stekelman, Betty Tamblyn, Bernard Burgoyne, Aggrey Burke and Newcross colleagues, George Crawford and colleagues, Patricia Fletchman, and Beulah Coombs.

Many thanks also to Kirsty Hall and to Duncan Barford of Rebus Press, without whose careful work and support my manuscript would not have become a book.

Finally, special thanks are due to my children, for putting up with me whilst I worked.

A NOTE ON TEXTS

Quotations and references to Freud are given according to the *Standard Edition of the Complete Psychological Works of Sigmund Freud*. 24 Vols. Translated and edited by James Strachey in collaboration with Anna Freud, assisted by Alix Strachey and Alan Tyson. London: The Hogarth Press and the Institute of Psycho-Analysis; New York: Norton, 1953-1974.

Mental Slavery

Psychoanalytic Studies of Caribbean People

by

Barbara Fletchman Smith

First published in 2000 by Rebus Press

Reprinted in 2003 by
H. Karnac (Books) Ltd.
6 Pembroke Buildings
London NW10 6RE

British Library Cataloguing in Publication Data
A C.I.P. for this book is available from the British Library

ISBN: 1 85575 908 X
www.karnacbooks.com

Printed & bound by Antony Rowe Ltd, Eastbourne

CONTENTS

Introduction

Slavery was a catastrophe for Africans and for Africa.

This book focuses on British people of Caribbean origin, who are suffering from varying degrees of psychological stress. The inescapable reality of a past which includes the trauma of slavery has an important influence upon this distress. However, the very idea that slavery and its aftermath might play a role in an individual's psychological state raises a lot of discomfort. This idea—on one side—causes people to feel they are being accused of barbarism, or else—on the other side—that they are the victims of permanent damage. Any examination of the traumatic consequences of slavery and its aftermath is thus fraught with difficulties.

Slaves were not supposed to have feelings, yet slavery formed the entire basis of Caribbean and American society. To my mind, then, trauma on a massive scale has been handed down through the generations, is still being handed down, and is hard to express and conceptualise. Nevertheless the way in which this happens can be observed in how individuals relate to themselves and to others.

I begin from the position that slavery was damaging for *everyone* concerned with it. As in all situations in which there are perpetrators and victims, it is what the victims do in their own minds with the horrors they experience that—to a large extent—determines the future state of mind of that individual. This explains why some people not only survived, but have thrived in spite of the experience of slavery. Others have not been so fortunate.

Many people, over the centuries, were saved from psychosis by strong religious beliefs. However, in the twentieth century, *psychology* now occupies the place in our lives left vacant by the decline of religion. Psychoanalysis—the study of the unconscious part of the mind—is, decidedly, not a religion. It has taught us what can be gained from looking beneath the surface, and this also entails looking *backwards*. It is by studying the past of the individual that the present within him or her begins to make sense.

Freud's discovery of the unconscious made it possible to begin to question European man's certainty of his 'rationality'. This self-assurance dates back to the eighteenth century, a time at which the dominant European culture became strongly identified with 'rationality', considered the best quality bequeathed by fifth century imperial Athens. Irrationality, on the other hand, was consigned to 'the other'—those on the margins of society or outside it. The contribution of psychoanalysis to this state of affairs has been a systematic description and problematisation of this 'splitting'. It has brought back to us the Euripidean possibility of the rational alongside the irrational, the uncivilised within the civilised. Psychoanalysis locates both within the same individual and within the same society.

Psychoanalysis should not be rejected because it took root in nineteenth century Vienna rather than elsewhere. It could—instead—be examined for its usefulness to people from a variety of backgrounds. Within any cultural or social group there will be individuals for whom psychoanalytic psychotherapy will be the most appropriate form of treatment for psychological disorders. Psychoanalysis and psychotherapy do not possess the answers to all problems, and neither do any other particular forms of therapy. However, it does seem to me that psychoanalysis is one of the most useful tools in existence, at present, for the understanding of human beings beneath their surface aspects.

In this book, I recognise the influence of western thinking on people of Caribbean background—myself included—and I accept that there is more than one way of understanding anything. Indeed, one of the advantages of coming from a society in which a dominant system of values has been imposed from outside, from the centre of the British Empire, is that this means one becomes quickly attuned to the possibility of other possibilities.

For instance, in Western European thinking a split between mind and body persists, which can cause quite serious difficulties when it comes to understanding the communications of some patients. Quite often, patients will present psychological distress in a physical way, and consequently will often get no further than seeing a medical doctor, or perhaps an initial assessment session with a psychotherapist. We shall examine instances of this in some detail.

However, these are difficulties which can be overcome within the profession. There is no single set of rules for working with patients from a Caribbean background. This is because people of this background are like everyone else, in the sense that they are—first and foremost—individuals. No single theoretical approach is more well-suited to them. The enemy is, rather, fundamentalism of any sort. In fundamentalism we lose sight of the worth of the individual, and of the true spirit of enquiry. If we want to define the difference between this group of patients and others, then it has to do with what has been passed down of the experience of slavery and its aftermath.

Among the legacies of slavery, for instance, is *fear*. A patient's fear can easily be underestimated, yet it must be recognised that this fear is distinct from anxiety *because it is likely to relate to a real rather than a phantasised past*.[1] When horrors occur in the present to members of ethnic minority groups, then something of the horrific past can be activated in the individual, with serious consequences. Another legacy of slavery—and its aftermath of racial discrimination—is a distortion of the relations between Caribbean men and women. This continues to affect the lives of their children. Another effect is the distortion of power-relations between men, based on skin colour; white men have great trouble sharing power with black men. Yet another consequence is a deep-rooted mistrust of women. To set these imbalances right entails work on the same scale as the abolition of slavery itself. Today, confrontation of the internalised slaver is just as important as it was to confront the external slaver. This entails immense castration anxiety, but to work through that anxiety is what distinguishes emancipation from mental slavery. What I mean by 'internalised slaver' will become clearer as we proceed.

Emotional pain can afflict anyone, but may become acute as a consequence of migration. The children of migrants are at particular risk, as migration may damage the family and destroy its capacity to repair itself. Sometimes—as has been mentioned—psychological pain expresses itself in a physical way, and becomes physically painful. Psychotherapeutic and psychodynamic work can help to unravel what belongs where. It can provide a relationship in which worries, concerns and deep fears can be privately explored and become better understood. Family worries may have endured for generations, in a relatively contained manner, but the stress of migration, caused by separation and feelings of loss, can upset the sense of balance in the life of an individual.

Despite being born in the UK or USA, young people from a Caribbean background are nevertheless strongly influenced by Caribbean culture in its widest sense. For a time, in England in the 1970s, there was a rift between the generations, born of disillusionment. Each of the generations living in England had very different life experiences and expectations. This has now—to a large extent—been healed, as a consequence of several factors: the perception of external threats to the community as a whole (such as increased racial attacks and murders, and economic deprivation); shared experiences of hardship; and also because, over time, families of three generations have formed: grandparents are now living in England, and are able to make a contribution to the care and upbringing of children.

British children of Caribbean origin who do not have available to them a granny or good granny substitute often miss out on love. This is particularly badly needed in a climate of busy working parents on relatively low incomes, of single mothers, and of racial hostility. Schools—especially nursery schools—could be a lot more imaginative in helping small children who need laps to sit on. A patient, first generation British-born, once told me that on meeting her granny for the first time, during a visit to the Caribbean when she was twelve-years-old, she thought to herself: '*this* is the person I've been waiting for!' The patient observed that her mother, at the same time, underwent: 'a huge change in energy and determination... as if she had been converted'. This should give us an idea of the sheer extent of the loss inflicted by migration. Children grow up with this sense that something is missing, but do not know what it is. Despite these difficulties, however, migration has been a good thing for most people. Difficulties of all kinds—economic, cultural, political—stand in the way of making best use of available opportunities, but it is at least possible that these will be rectified in the future. Ultimately, however, it is the psychological aspect of these difficulties which interests me here.

* * *

The chapters which follow are divided into two parts. Part One is concerned with historical background, psychoanalytic theory, and the nature of psychotic illness. This includes working definitions of psychosis, neurosis and borderline states, and also a reading of a novel—Caribbean writer Roy Heath's *The Murderer*—in order to explore the relationship between paranoia and schizophrenia, through this account of a young man's psychotic breakdown. Part One concludes with an application of psychoanalysis to a study of the central character —'Galton Flood'—in Heath's novel. Part Two goes on to explore the origins of mental distress in adulthood, including chapters on the psychological vicissitudes of a male baby, and of a child within a dysfunctional extended family. The final chapters concern individual cases of neurotic illness.

PART ONE

Historical and Theoretical

Chapter One

Slavery: The Historical Background

Before taking a look at the inside of patients of Caribbean origin, I think it would be appropriate to take a look outside, at the historical connections between Africans in the Caribbean, and the British.[2]

I have grouped together the different countries of the Caribbean, but in the full knowledge that they are very different from one another. To me their differences are less important than their similarities because the people of these countries—together with African-Americans—share a historical past.

The terms 'British of Caribbean origin', 'African-Caribbean', 'Afro-British', 'Black British', 'Black English', 'Scots or Welsh of Caribbean origin' are all used currently to describe the group of men and women upon which I wish to focus. The wide variety of definitions is part of a wider process of re-assembling identities, currently taking place in the post-empire, post-independence period. Indeed, 'people of Caribbean origin' also include the descendants of indentured labourers from Europe, Asia and elsewhere, and Caribbean people who migrated to the USA will have experiences in common with those who migrated to the UK. The majority of the population in most Caribbean countries, however, continues to be ethnic African.[3] So although I am focusing upon people of *African* origin, I am aware that most people from the Caribbean are racially mixed to some degree. It is true to say that they are *predominantly* ethnically African, and their descendants in Britain are also viewed as such. In a climate in which racism thrives, one runs the risks of 'singling out' this group of people as a 'problem'. However, this is a risk I am prepared to take. By damaging others, people also damage themselves, and I suspect that if I were to focus on the children of former slave-owners, then I would discover traumas there too. In the making of empires, it is inevitable that crimes will be committed.

People of Caribbean origin share a history that begins with slavery and indenture, but—of course—the history of the peo-

ple of Africa extends back much further. The relationship
between Europeans and their African neighbours—for it should
be remembered that the two continents are geographically less
than ten miles apart—is one of exploitation. The development of
Europe was at the expense of Africa. This is despite the fact that,
as human beings, we have the capacity to shape our history in a
non-exploitative way.

Britain in the fourteenth century was poor in comparison
with the rest of the world. It was this that drove its people outwards in pursuit of wealth. The culmination of the efforts of the
heroes in English history—men such as Sir Francis Drake in the
sixteenth century, for instance—was the establishment of plantation societies in the Americas and the Caribbean, by the beginning of the eighteenth century.

European involvement in the slave trade has to be set alongside Arab involvement, and African co-operation and resistance.
When Egypt fell to the Arabs in AD 641, a gradual process of
colonisation by Africans began. The Arabs, for centuries,
imposed their Islamic religion from the north of the African continent downwards, replacing the dominant religions of
Animism and Christianity. There were Christians in Africa long
before the British ever went there. Many wars were fought, in
which African slaves were taken, and Arabs were the instigators
of these wars. Africans also indulged in the taking of slaves
from other African states.

Both Europeans and Arabs used their religion as the justification of their actions—as the whole of mankind always has.
However, if sub-Saharan Africans had been more willing to
allow reforms within their societies, they might have been able
to eradicate slavery within their own nations—and outside—
much earlier. Yet equally, had they chosen instead to fight to the
death in an attempt to halt the push of the Arabs and Europeans
further and further into the continent, then they might have suffered a fate similar to that of the American Indians or Australian
Aborigines. We will never know what might have happened
otherwise, but it is interesting to speculate. Greed, hatred, and
love are universal human attributes, each in more plentiful supply at a certain time than at other times. What is clear, however,

is that as time went on the Europeans came to possess superior tools of war—due to the wealth created through continuation of the slave trade itself—and which they were very happy to put to use. It must be remembered, however, that the slave trade endured for hundreds of years.

The slave trade financed the 'high culture' of eighteenth century England, and provided the financial base for the industrialisation of the United Kingdom. To my knowledge, however, the existence of the slave trade features in the literature of the nineteenth century only in a heavily coded fashion. An example of this can be seen in the work of Charles Dickens—specifically, in the character Tom Gradgrind from the novel *Hard Times* (published 1853). Dickens was 41-years-old at the time he wrote this novel in which Tom, the Gradgrind family's son and heir, ends up having to evade exposure as a thief by dressing as a 'blackamoor' (a European construction of an African) in a circus (Dickens 1982). This disguise might be read as an appropriate course of action to avoid detection. However, to me it reads instead as the author's unconscious acknowledgement that the real thieves are not the 'blackamoors'. I take the 'blackamoor' as representing black foreign people who lost land and freedom to the British. The circus people in the novel appear as a combined representation of the arts, the working classes, and the dispossessed in general. Dickens could have chosen a different disguise for Tom, but by putting him into the skin of 'the other' he attempts to put his audience also in the position of the 'blackamoor'. Despite the lack of explicit references in nineteenth-century literature, Victorians were very aware of slaves and slavery, and thus were likely to respond strongly to the plight of Tom who—by adopting the 'blackamoor' disguise—simultaneously loses his own land and freedom. Dickens himself held deeply Christian values, which were mostly in direct opposition to the institutionally practised 'Christianity' in Victorian society.

By the time the Industrial Revolution was complete, the freedom of the slaves had become an option. The British Empire was by no means the only Empire built upon slavery, but it was the first from which there was no hope of gaining freedom with the passage of time. There was no way out except resistance. In the end it became too expensive for the British to maintain slavery, because of the continuous necessity to suppress perpetual revolts on the plantations. Also, industrialisation brought with it a need for markets for the goods being produced. Consequently, the slave trade lost its supremacy, and as the demand for slaves steadily decreased the supply itself could finally be abandoned.

Britain was the chief European country involved in the organisation of the slave trade. It conducted its operations from three main centres: the ports of London, Bristol and Liverpool. Indeed, the municipal development of Bristol and Liverpool was entirely dependent on slavery. In turn, the Caribbean plantation owners became extremely wealthy men, and used their money to buy power and influence in the British parliament and aristocracy. It was this power against which the black and white Abolitionists had to struggle, yet, even as the slave trade went into decline, the plantation owners and traders received huge sums of compensation for the loss of their livelihood.

The Abolitionist movement grew out of eighteenth-century Humanism. There were many decent British and African people who abhorred the trade in human lives, and who made its abolition their life-long task.[4] In much the same way, today, there are decent people making history through their daily work towards racial justice and equality.

In the Caribbean, the abolition of slavery was succeeded by the importation of the indentured labour of Europeans (mainly Portuguese), East Indians, Chinese, Arabs, and others. Africans had a different relationship to the land from these new arrivals; many Africans could not wait to escape from the country altogether. At this time it was very difficult to obtain enough land of one's own to make a living. Slavery thus passed through Abolition to Emancipation, and then into the era of Colonialism. Independence from Colonialism followed in the 1960s.

The people who arrived in the Caribbean after the Africans entered a society which already possessed an established Creole language. They had to learn how to speak both English and Creole. In the process, many of these non-English-speaking people lost their original languages. At the time of slavery,

Caribbean society was rigidly structured, with the plantation owners at the top, and the people of mixed blood—from unions between Europeans and Africans—forming the next layer. Africans were the bottom layer of this society, the most numerous group. Among the Europeans in the British colonies there was also a split between land-owning, mostly English-speaking Protestants, and landless, largely non-English-speaking Roman Catholics. The latter, in time, acquired land.

From the mix produced by these processes emerged the modern Caribbean men and women, with practically no links to the original, indigenous Caribbeans. The bulk of the people were also officially disconnected from the African countries of their ancestors, until after Independence□. The Caribbean plantocracy retained their connection with Europe. Continual racial inter-mixing of the many different peoples has ensured that there are no 'pure' Africans descended from the original African slaves—that is, 'pure' as far as this term can ever have any meaning. African languages, beliefs and customs which had been transported to the Caribbean with the slaves were either lost completely, or have lain buried, waiting to surface. The customs of the different peoples have combined together over time, and have become transformed into a culture which is now uniquely 'Caribbean'.

Many academics have taken on the challenge of exploring the roots of language, in order to attempt to reconnect with the past. Language itself is the mark of a specific culture. The Creole language developed over the centuries as an exclusively oral language, firstly between the slaves who originated from different nations and spoke various languages, and then between the slaves and their owners. The slaves were forbidden to speak their African languages amongst themselves purely as a means of controlling them.

Creole drew upon African as well as European languages. There are three different Creole languages spoken within the Caribbean. This is due to the way in which different European countries with their different languages ruled over the various countries in the region. The speaking of English (and also French and Spanish) in preference to Creole was viewed as the mark of education and class throughout Caribbean society for centuries. Along with the English language, English culture was also absorbed. Only in the second half of the twentieth century—the post-colonial period—have these societies become comfortable enough with themselves to claim Creole as an oral and a written language. Published writers from the region often use English, French or Spanish as well as Creole, and Creole-English dictionaries have since been published.

However, some ambivalence remains over claiming Creole as a fully distinct language in its own right—as might be imagined from the circumstances we have reviewed so far. It seems highly probable that psychological disturbance would have arisen in individuals forbidden to speak their own language, in slavery times. During the migration of Caribbean people this century a similar inhibition against using language might also have occurred, which would affect the capacity of some children to develop language and symbol formation. Most probably, this will have been associated with the occurrence of severely depressed states in the parents. It can easily be imagined how the failure of the processes of verbal self-expression must endanger a person's mental health, especially if alternative modes of expression cannot be found. I suspect that this state of affairs has been partly responsible for a great deal of ill-health. The loss of familiar ways of communicating, and of loved ones with whom to communicate, was as bad as the loss of familiar foods and climate.

It is interesting to note that the children of Caribbean migrants, regardless of their country of origin, who live in the inner-city areas of the UK and USA, have developed languages of their own which they use to express their separateness and exclusivity. This can be viewed as an unconscious reclamation of something that was lost. However, when the language used by a person to express intimacy is not understood by outsiders, then serious problems will arise when professionals attempt to make meaningful contact with the individuals concerned. It is known that this process frequently occurs, and has fundamental implications for any form of inter-personal work in which words assume importance.

I have entered into these historical details because I think that history has fundamentally influenced the way people of European and African origin treat one another today, and also the way in which each regards themselves. Slavery severely traumatised people—to such an extent that it affected people's capacity to procreate. Terror, perpetual fear, cruel abuse and gruelling work were the order of the day. Slave women frequently took control of their own fertility by killing their children, in order to prevent them from becoming slaves themselves. Following Emancipation and Independence, a population which was unable to rise in number during slavery began to swell dramatically once people felt in control of their own lives. The political significance of Emancipation and Independence was of great importance to people of African origin; it seemed inevitable that migration would become an appealing option.

Alongside migration, there is the legacy of the continuing struggle for equality as human beings. I very much doubt that the majority of British people have yet caught up with the significance of Emancipation, its potential for good. The loss of an Empire built upon slavery is something of which to be proud; however, it is not possible to feel this without a period of mourning. This—hopefully—will be worked through in much the same way as more personal matters need to be worked through, and is a process hindered by high levels of denial. For instance, it is a fact that the slave trade created the United States of America as we know it today. Many people do not know this. Some, of course, do not *wish* to know it. Similarly, schoolchildren, taken to visit Ironbridge in Shropshire, England—the birthplace of the Industrial Revolution—are not helped to make the connection between the rush to smelt iron and the slave trade. Nowadays much money is spent on promoting English heritage, but it does not include this particular bit of history. While this attitude persists, people of African origin are likely to be blamed for all sorts of imagined wrongs. It is, as yet, far from certain whether the nation can find a different way of being from that based on the notion of a 'top' and a 'bottom'—which is the same as that on which slavery and colonialism was based.

The European mind, evidently, is as much in need of Emancipation as the Caribbean mind. Attacks on migrants—whether on a personal or governmental level—are uncreative, but also a terrible waste of energy as people have migrated from the beginning of time, and will go on doing so, whenever they think there is the possibility of a better life elsewhere.

Africans have lived in Britain since Roman times, which—as we have already reminded ourselves—is not surprising, given the close proximity of the African and European continents, physically less than ten miles apart. From the fifteenth century onwards—and particularly during the reign of Elizabeth I (1558-1603)—much was recorded of their presence. Some Africans came directly to Britain as free men, and others as slaves. Children have—for centuries—been sent to Britain to be educated. Some Africans were brought as slaves directly from Africa, or from the Caribbean or America. It was not unusual for Africans to be seen in England throughout the seventeenth and eighteenth centuries. The practice of keeping slaves was largely undertaken abroad, in the new American colonies and the Caribbean. Indeed, slaves were vital to the establishment of these colonies and were regarded as status symbols by the English aristocracy, who were only too willing to have their portraits painted with their slaves in attendance. There seems to have been no general shame or guilt at this time attached to the chaining and collaring of human beings, yet there have—for centuries—been black and white voices in England raised in protest against this way of treating people.

During the twentieth century the British Empire began to dissolve, as a result of Independence movements and two world wars. At the same time there was a migration of people from the Caribbean and elsewhere to the UK and to North America. People migrated in the expectation of better lives; thus most were economic migrants, like the Europeans of the nineteenth century. At that time British and other European people had migrated to the Americas, the Caribbean, Africa, Australia, New Zealand and India. Nearly three million people left the UK between 1853 and 1880, to live overseas in the New World because—as the liberal historian Geoffrey Best put it—'their country became incapable of offering them the means of living by their own labour' (Best 1979: 147). These events are recorded in the paintings 'The Last of England' (1852-3) by Ford Madox Brown, and 'The Emigrant's Last Sight of Home' (1858) by Richard Redgrave.[5] Economic conditions in the Caribbean during the twentieth century had a similar effect on the people living there.

So far, I have attempted to sketch the connection between Africa, Britain and the Caribbean, and to trace the journey of Caribbean migrants to Britain. I am not concerned in the book with the issue of race relations as such—with how British people of one hue relate to those of another—although this will, necessarily, be somewhere in the background. Migration has consequences—both for those left behind, and for the countries in which migrants arrive. Migration to the very centre of what had been the British Empire, of people whose forebears had been enslaved in Africa and taken to the Caribbean, was evidently a very serious matter. Firstly, it involved the loss of important attachments to loved ones who might never be seen again. Secondly, it meant the breaking of traditional ties of loyalty to a culture. The disruption of personal ties disturbed the individual's whole being, which sometimes took years to repair—or sometimes was never repaired at all. This is not unique to people of African origin. What was unique in their case, however, was the past they carried with them, of having had their lives massively disrupted when they themselves were traded in exchange for worldly goods. Migration to Britain clarified the deeper meaning of slavery. Slavery meant the subjugation of those who were different. Slavery left almost as much fear of 'the other' in the minds of the slavers as in the minds of the enslaved.

However, my concern is mainly with how black British individuals from a Caribbean background get along with *themselves*—that is, how they relate with the different parts of themselves, and how they relate to their families and others.

Chapter Two

Psychosis and Neurosis: the Theoretical Background

By applying psychoanalysis to the study of psychotic break-down, Freud opened up a whole new avenue of understanding.

In 1911 he published 'Psycho-Analytic Notes upon an Autobiographical Account of a Case of Paranoia (Dementia Paranoides)', in which he set out his most detailed formulation of paranoia. He based this theory upon a reading of Daniel Paul Schreber's autobiographical study, *Memoirs of my Nervous Illness* (1955), although he had formulated his ideas well before coming across the case of Schreber. Schreber's book started out as a series of notes, initially intended to help his wife understand his condition. But then he concluded that his experience of psy-chotic illness—or 'nervous illness', as he called it—might inter-est a larger audience.

I will not describe in detail Freud's study of Schreber. However, Freud's major conclusion from his encounter with the case was that psychoanalysis can provide an understanding of psychosis as well as neurosis. Schreber's *Memoirs* provided Freud with a vehicle for expressing his views on paranoia. He traced the ways in which paranoia can turn into something more serious—the total disintegration of a psychotic break-down.

Before proceeding, we must define some terms. Definitions are related directly to theoretical positions, which are manifold. My definitions are, therefore, necessarily selective, according to the aims and purposes of this study.

What is 'psychosis' and what is 'neurosis'? Generally speak-ing, the psychoses are those illnesses commonly and collective-ly described as 'madness'. They include paranoia, manic depressive states, and the schizophrenias—which are generally thought to comprise three types.

Freud, like his colleague Karl Abraham (1949), believed that psychosis was a regressive state in which the individual proves unable to transfer his sexual drive onto the outside world and away from his own body—in other words, this is a failure of 'transference'. Rickman (1957) described psychosis in similar terms—as a difficulty in the shift from autoerotism to object relations.

Paranoia, meanwhile, is characterised by a system of delusions, usually unaccompanied by any weakening of the intellect, and usually without any reduction of interest in the external world (cf. Freud 1911: 75). Paranoid delusions can be of a persecutory, grandiose, or erotomaniac type. Paranoid ideas, as Robert Waelder points out, cannot be corrected by experience. He suggests that:

> Many systems of thought which have profoundly influenced the course of history have been more or less akin to paranoid systems. One may even say that history is, to a large extent, the outcome of two forces, viz., on the one hand the process of learning from experience, the struggle for a better adjustment to, or a better mastery of, reality, both natural and man-made, and on the other hand the ever continuing rise of paranoid structures. (Waelder 1976: 208)

Schizophrenia is generally regarded as the most regressive of the psychoses (cf. Freud 1911: 76). In schizophrenia there is total withdrawal of interest from the external world—there is no inclination at all towards object love. According to Freud, the fixation point in schizophrenia is situated earlier than in paranoia, and 'must lie somewhere at the beginning of the course of development from auto-erotism to object love' (Freud 1911: 77). Schizophrenia is characterised by splitting, and by hallucinatory defences (both auditory and visual). The schizophrenic delusion, according to Freud, 'is found applied like a patch over the place where originally a rent had appeared in the ego's relation to the external world' (Freud 1924b: 151). The term 'schizophrenia' was first employed in 1911 by Eugen Bleuler.

Robert Bak (1971) provides a graphic portrayal of what happens to someone who develops this illness. He describes a withdrawal from the environment, marked passivity, sparse contact with others and a lack of initiative, leading to dropping out of school, work, or friendships, withdrawal into the home or idling about in public places, and an existence characterised solely by sleeping, eating and watching TV—or by not getting up in the morning at all. In addition, schizophrenics are preoccupied with their own body, and experience strange hypochondriacal sensations frequently related to problems with sexual identity. They demonstrate poor control of aggression and unprovoked fits of rage, as well as unpremeditated and inappropriate sexual approaches, and mild forms of thought disorder—especially an inability to concentrate. Often their thoughts become audible to them as external voices.

Theories of psychosis and neurosis

Freud's study of Schreber's *Memoirs* was a huge breakthrough in the understanding of psychotic breakdown in general, and of paranoia in particular. For a long time, Freud's ideas were not examined critically—partly out of respect for the great man, but also because *Memoirs* was not available in English. These days, however, there is no shortage of re-readings of both works.

Although Freud's paper is still acclaimed, there are many alternative ways of understanding paranoia, the case of Schreber, and homosexuality—which, according to Freud, plays a key role in paranoid delusions.[6] What is forgotten in many of the criticisms of Freud's work is that a great number of the concepts taken for granted in psychoanalysis today were simply not available to Freud at the time. Also unavailable to Freud were Schreber's medical records, and documents relating to members of his family (Niederland 1963; Baumeyer 1956). Nevertheless, Freud's work was underpinned by the concepts of the unconscious, defence, and mental conflict, and these have stood the test of time.

Freud concluded that Schreber's illness was the consequence of an outburst of homosexual libido, which had been vigorously defended against. Freud described this in terms of various contradictions of an unconscious proposition: 'I (a man) love him (a man)'. This proposition can be contradicted in various ways, which give rise to delusions of persecution or of jealousy.

In cases of persecution, the contradiction runs as follows: 'I do not love him—I hate him'. The act of contradiction is unconscious, yet the internal perception that 'I *hate* him' is transformed—by projection onto the other—into 'he hates *me*'. As Freud put it: 'we now see, that what was abolished internally returns from without' (Freud 1911: 71). This process is also known as denial. It justifies the paranoiac's hostility. He feels entitled to be hostile, because he is persecuted by the other. At the same time, he is building a system of thinking which destroys reality, in order to rationalise his beliefs and convictions. For Freud, then, the motive underlying paranoid delusion was the defence against homosexuality.

Another conclusion drawn by Freud—which would certainly be disputed by the school of object relations, in particular—was that Schreber's mental conflict arose from the Oedipus complex. Freud stresses the genital level of the conflict, yet also refers to Schreber as fixated at a *narcissistic* stage of libidinal development—which suggests a pre-Oedipal conflict. As Freud sees it, Schreber's conflict mostly concerns unconscious homosexual love for his father and brother. However, at a later stage in his paper, Freud makes it quite clear that in schizophrenia the link between paranoia and homosexuality does not necessarily apply:

> ...it is not at all likely that homosexual impulsions, which are so frequently—partly invariably—to be found in paranoia, play an equally important part in the aetiology of that far more comprehensive disorder, dementia praecox. (Freud 1911: 77)

Freud's paper on Schreber, then, does not provide the last word on paranoia, but opens up a whole host of questions.

For a long time, re-readings of the Schreber study continued this emphasis on the Oedipal level of mental conflict in Schreber, until publication of work by Spring (1939), Knight (1940), Baumeyer (1956) and Niederland (1951, 1959a, 1959b, 1960). Spring draws attention to the pregenital nature of Schreber's destructive fantasies. Knight comments that

Schreber's conflict with homosexual impulses is due to the ambivalent, pregenital, anal-sadistic quality of homosexual love. Baumeyer unearthed Schreber's medical records and family history, which supply information about his mother. She is described in these documents as nervous and subject to changes in mood, whilst Schreber's father is characterised as a disturbed man who suffered from obsessional neurosis with homicidal impulses. Such a pair of parents may have had trouble providing for the psychological well-being of their children, as Niederland suggests.

Re-readings of the paper by object relations theorists reflect subsequent developments in psychoanalysis. These writers stress the importance of the relationship between Schreber and his mother in its very earliest stages. W.R.D. Fairbairn (1956) suggests that 'if the mother-imago is conspicuous by its absence in Schreber's phantasies, this may be a measure of his mother's importance rather than otherwise' (Fairbairn 1956). Fairbairn also attributed Schreber's illness to a horror of the primal scene, with its resultant hatred of the mother for her unfaithfulness to the child. Melanie Klein—on the other hand—focused upon the infant's earliest anxieties. She emphasised the baby's greed and destructiveness, its envy of the mother rather than its neediness. Her exposition of the paranoid-schizoid position—as the first phase of psychic development, which precedes the depressive position and the early stages of the Oedipus complex—helped to explain Schreber's difficulties in pre-Oedipal terms.

Donald Winnicott, like Klein, was also an object relations theorist, yet more sympathetic to the importance of the role of *deficit*. He was less interested in emphasising the infant's hostility and destructiveness, which Klein believed drove the child into constructing an internal object far more cruel than the actual, external object. Instead, Winnicott's work enables us to understand Schreber's psychotic breakdown in terms of a lack of 'good-enough' infant care. Niederland's research into the life-histories of members of the Schreber family provides evidence which corroborates this view (Niederland 1963). Winnicott suggests that whatever the baby does with the idea of the mother in its mind, it is the mother's job to neutralise this and thus bring the baby back to sanity (Winnicott 1960).

Ida Macalpine and Richard Hunter, in their introduction to their translation of Schreber's *Memoirs*, also locate Schreber's difficulties in the pre-Oedipal period. They suggest that doubt and uncertainty concerning sexual identification—rather than passive homosexual wishes—was the cause of his illness. His psychosis (according to them) embodies a quest to procreate, in the context of a marriage to a wife who produced only stillborn babies (Schreber 1955).

In 1924, Freud differentiated between neurosis and psychosis as follows:

> ...in a neurosis the ego, in its dependence on reality, suppresses a piece of the id (of instinctual life), whereas in a psychosis, this same ego, in the service of the id, withdraws from a piece of reality. Thus for a neurosis the decisive factor would be the predominance of the influence of reality, whereas for a psychosis it would be the predominance of the id. In a psychosis, a loss of reality would necessarily be present, whereas in a neurosis, it would seem, this loss would be avoided... (Freud 1924a: 183)

The term 'neurosis' predates Freud. Since the second half of the eighteenth century, it meant 'a disease of the nerves'. In the nineteenth century neurosis was believed to be due to functional disturbances of the nervous system which were unaccompanied by structural changes (cf. Ellenberger 1970: 240-6). Freud, who began his career as a neurologist, found that neurosis was not a disease of the nervous system, but a purely mental disorder. He regarded neurosis as that which happens in the mind when the individual has to deal with frustration. He believed that people fell ill with neurosis as they attempted to adapt to and meet the demands of reality, due to a conflict between the ego and the libido or sexual drives.[7]

Freud identified three common features in the sexuality of neurotics: the forceful repression of a strong sexual drive; a sexuality with a perverse quality; and a sexuality with infantile characteristics. Later, he added aggressivity as yet another common feature. He identified two basic categories of neurosis: hysterical and obsessional.

Today, neurosis is understood as partly determined by infant and childhood experiences, and partly by what the child does in his mind with these experiences. Freud himself initially believed that hysteria was caused by sexual abuse inflicted by an adult and passively suffered by the child. However, he later qualified this point of view, as expressed in the famous letter to his friend Wilhelm Fliess, dated 21st September 1897 (Masson 1985: 264-6).

Following from Freud, who regarded neurosis as an illness which can be cured, Jacques Lacan saw it as a *structure* (one of three, the others being psychosis and perversion) which cannot be altered. He viewed what we call 'mental health' as an illusory ideal of wholeness, which can never be attained because the individual (or 'subject') is essentially split. The Lacanian subject who suffers from neurosis (hysteria) is understood as asking a fundamental question about his or her sex; the obsessional neurotic, meanwhile, is presumed to be questioning his very existence—is he 'to be or not to be'. A similar view of neurosis is presented by Ella Freeman Sharpe. She defined it as not knowing what to do with one's life, at a fundamental level (Sharpe 1950). The aim of Lacanian psychoanalysis is the modification of *the subject's position in relation to* the neurosis. For the Freudian, in contrast, the original aim of psychoanalysis was to find the causes of the illness and—through psychotherapy—to alleviate the symptoms. In other words, 'transforming... hysterical misery into common unhappiness' (Breuer & Freud 1893-1895: 304-5).

As mentioned above, Melanie Klein's work focuses upon the earliest infantile and childhood experiences, rather than placing the emphasis upon the Freudian Oedipus complex. Klein thought that envy was heavily implicated in neurosis and psychosis. She believed that both neurosis and psychosis are parts of each individual's mental make-up. Her notion of 'positions' which can be adopted at any time throughout life—the *paranoid-schizoid position* (the earliest) and the *depressive position*—effectively situated both psychotic and neurotic functioning within each individual.

It is this framework of thought which makes it easier to accommodate the notion of yet another category of mental disorder—the *borderline* disorder. Theorists who operate within a system in which there are three definite structures (neurosis, psychosis, perversion—the Lacanians), or only two (neurosis, psychosis—the Freudians) find it unnecessary to accept borderline disorders as a separate category of illness. The first writer to describe what some now understand as 'borderline' phenomena was W.R.D. Fairbairn (1940). Melanie Klein's 'Notes on Some Schizoid Mechanisms' (1946) followed a few years after.

The borderline patient presents a complex mixture of symptoms. The same patient may, from moment to moment, present symptoms that are neurotic—perhaps even only mildly neurotic in the midst of severely psychotic symptoms. Otto Kernberg in a classic paper, 'Borderline Personality Organisation' (1967), makes the point that borderline disorders are described in altogether different terms—for instance: 'psychotic characters'; '"as if" personalities'; 'preschizophrenic personality structure'; 'severe ego distortions'—all implying the notion of borderline *states* rather than fixed symptoms.

Theories of childhood development

Psychoanalytic studies of childhood development, and clinical work with adults, throw light on the origins of psychosis and neurosis. Accordingly, I will now spend a short while examining various psychoanalytic theories of child development, and of its relation to psychosis.

Freud's theory of development suggests a progressive working-through from autoerotism to narcissism to object love. There is also a progression through the oral, anal, phallic and genital phases of sexual satisfaction. Object love emerges at the phallic stage, yet at each of these stages there is the possibility of a fixation-point occurring.

Freud also proposed a unique theory of love—fundamental to psychoanalysis—namely, the Oedipus complex. All human beings have to face the struggle of passing through the Oedipus complex. In his case study of 'Little Hans', Freud describes the trials and tribulations of a little boy experiencing castration anxiety and negotiating the Oedipus complex (Freud 1909). The complex arises, unconsciously, from the triangular structure of the relationship between mother, father and child. Within this triangle the child feels driven to try to preserve the original love-bond with the mother, by wishing to eliminate the father. Failure to negotiate the Oedipus complex successfully leaves the individual vulnerable to illness. One of the consequences of denying the psychic existence of the father—or 'father function', as Lacan later described it—in the triangular relationship, is the engulfment of the child by the mother. It is this state of affairs which increases the risk of psychosis. Neurotics, unlike psychotics, pass through struggles of loving and hating, but in the end retain their grasp on reality. They cope with the struggle to accept the father's existence and his position, and make their way through the Oedipus complex.

Jacques Lacan, who conducted a formidable re-reading of Freud's study on Schreber, took Freud's ideas on psychosis further. He suggested that two conditions work together to produce a psychosis. The first condition is that the individual possesses a psychotic mental structure (as opposed to one of the other two structures—neurotic or perverse).[8] The second condition is that the father is not internally symbolised—that is, he is not integrated into the subject's symbolic universe because, on the contrary, he has been expelled from it. This state of affairs Lacan describes as 'foreclosure'. In Lacanian terms, foreclosure implies that the phallus is expelled along with the father. Lacan conceives of the mental field as three interacting 'orders'—the symbolic, the imaginary, and the real.[9] The result of foreclosure (the expulsion of the father or phallus from internal symbolisation) results in a hole in the symbolic order, through which hallucinations and delusions may enter. This mechanism exceeds ordinary denial. What was not symbolised returns instead 'in the real', as an hallucination. In effect, foreclosure restricts the image of the father to the imaginary and the real, and excludes it from the symbolic.[10]

Thus Lacan provides a convincing explanation why some people become psychotic and others do not. He suggests the answer lies in the mental structure of the individual or subject. Someone with a neurotic structure can never become psychotic—that is, develop delusions or experience hallucinations. Only someone who has a psychotic structure to begin with will 'foreclose'.

The development of the Lacanian infant begins with the task of recognising his own body, during the 'mirror stage' (which occurs between six to eighteen months). By identifying with the image of himself in the mirror, or the image of himself mirrored back to him by other people, the child begins to feel an illusory sense of unity. By recognising his own image and falling in love with it, he moves from an autoerotic to a narcissistic stage. Lacan suggests that at this point the ego is constructed from the child's image of itself. The ego is formed at this point of alienation from oneself and fascination with one's image instead. Thus, there is a basic lack of being at the heart of the human subject. It is in the image—the first organised form—that the individual identifies himself. Commonly, the ego is regarded as an autonomous entity, but this is only an illusion. Fragmentation is never far away. Lacan repeatedly emphasises the ego's ability to misconstrue things, to refuse to accept the truth. When the child acquires language he attains the important stage of subjectivity. He can begin to represent his thoughts and feelings, including his essential lack of being as manifested in his wishes and desires.

Object relations theorists base their work on a different conception of the structure of the mind. However, their explanation of psychotic breakdown is not as radically different from that of Freud or Lacan as it at first appears.

Winnicott writes:

...before object relationships the state of affairs is this: that the unit is not the individual, the unit is an environment-individual set-up. The centre of gravity of the being does not start off in the individual. It is in the total set-up. By good-enough child care, technique, holding, and general management the shell becomes gradually taken over and the kernel (which has looked all the time like a human baby to us) can begin to be an individual. The beginning is potentially terrible because of the anxieties I have mentioned and because of the paranoid state that follows closely on the first integration, and also on the first instinctual moments, bringing to the baby, as they do a quite new meaning to object relationships. The good enough infant care technique neutralises the external persecutions and prevents the feelings of disintegration... (Winnicott 1952a: 99)

This statement demonstrates just how much responsibility Winnicott places on the mother for facilitating the infant's development. To him, the maternal function is crucial in the development of psychic processes. This is in stark contrast to Lacan's emphasis on the father function. The infant, according to Winnicott, passes through stages of absolute dependence, relative dependence, and then towards independence. He sees development in as *innate potential + environment*. The environment consists of the mother, supported by the baby's father and family. The Winnicottian mother thus provides an environment in which to nurture potential. She also provides herself as a reflective object which mirrors the infant. Winnicott's theory of the mirroring role of the mother was influenced by the work of Lacan. When the baby looks into the mother's face—Winnicott suggests—the baby sees itself. If the mother is unresponsive there are consequences: the baby adopts any number of strategies to cope with being ignored and thrown into chaos. Winnicott writes: 'If the mother's face is unresponsive, then a mirror is a thing to be looked at but not to be looked into' (Winnicott 1967: 132).

The most important developmental task facing both mother and infant is for the infant to be helped to become integrated and to become a separate being. The mother has to act as facilitator to the baby, facilitating transitions between the baby's illusion of oneness with the mother, of its being powerful enough to meet all its needs by itself; and the baby's acknowledgement of the mother's role in providing for his needs, of the mother as a separate person. Inability on the part of the mother to meet this challenge results in an infant who only sees how the mother feels, and is deprived of confirmation of his own feelings and sense of being. Winnicott links his ideas on good-enough mothering to the development of a true self, and of not good-enough mothering to the development of a false self (Winnicott 1962: 56-63). The creation of a false self is the road to psychotic illness.

Winnicott, as well as being an object relations theorist, was also associated with the British Independent school of psychoanalytic theory. Like other theorists of this school, he believed the mechanism of splitting (which is mobilised in the creation of a false self) entails that the individual will have difficulty integrating and feeling whole. In another paper—'Psychoses and Child Care' (1952b)—Winnicott elaborates on his view that a mother who is not good-enough directly causes psychosis in children and adults.

Melanie Klein's focus upon the infant's *own* conflicts emphasises how both contentment and fear can be experienced in relation to the very same object. The Kleinian infant has an object relationship from the very beginning of life. Initially this is a relationship with the mother's breast—a part-object, standing for the mother—which is split even further into 'good breast' and 'bad breast'. The good part is idealised, whilst the bad part becomes terrifyingly persecutory. The infant, from the very beginning (and, later, the adult) utilises the processes of introjection and projection to keep the good and bad parts widely apart. The infant is conceived as projecting its love, hatred, and all its other complex feelings into the breast. Strong aggressive instincts are also there from the very beginning of the infant's life, existing alongside the libidinal instincts, and thus producing ambivalence from the very start. Feelings of intense anxiety are also present, associated with the experiences of the object as persecutory.

Klein is interested in what the infant does in his own mind with that which he takes in from outside. Her theory of development is not linear—like Freud's. Instead—as we have seen—she employs the notion of 'positions'. The first, the paranoid-schizoid position, lasts for the first four months of life and is followed by the depressive position. According to Klein the individual can move from one to the other at any later stage of life, from childhood to old age. Klein suggests that the infant experiences the body as—firstly—in pieces, and only later as a whole. She believes that, in this earliest period,

> ...anxieties characteristic of psychosis arise which drive the ego to develop specific defence-mechanisms. In this period the fixation points for all psychotic disorders are to be found. The hypothesis led some people to believe that I regarded all infants as psychotic... (Klein 1946: 1)

The depressive position, however, evolves after the fourth month of life, and from this the infant moves to the early stages of the Oedipus complex. In the depressive position, anxiety concerns the loss of the internal and external whole object. Aggressive and libidinal instincts become focused on the whole object rather than part-objects, and the infant's anxiety is that the whole object might be destroyed and the mother lost as a result of its sadism. At this time the infant becomes concerned for its mother. It is a combination of these factors which make for the depressed feelings that arise in this position. The infant can only work through this position if its loving feelings predominate. When the infant feels loved and can love, it no longer has any need for the defences of the earlier, paranoid-schizoid position—denial, idealisation, splitting and omnipotence. According to Klein, the gap between the internal phantasy object and the external object now becomes more narrow. Love and hatred draw closer together than in the paranoid-schizoid position, and there is less intense sadism.

By the end of the depressive position, the child realises that the object can withstand its negative feelings, and will not reject the child because of them. The child can also experience the separatenenss of the object, and can mourn for the loss of the omnipotence which was part of the illusion of oneness with the object. In contrast, in both the paranoid-schizoid and depressive positions, there is a limit on the level of anxiety which can be tolerated by the infant before the infant becomes heavily reliant on the defences of splitting, idealisation and denial.

Klein's understanding of projection, one of the key mechanisms at work in paranoia, was developed from Freud's work on melancholia (Freud 1917), whilst her ideas on introjection were developed from the work of Abraham (1949). She draws together these two sets of notions in her paper on mourning and the failure to mourn (Klein 1940). However, her theory of projective identification (Klein 1946), brought something entirely new to the practice of psychoanalysis. Later, Klein was to claim that envy was deeply implicated in projective identification—that is, as a defence in which parts of the ego are forced into an object, in order to take over the contents of the object or to control it. Nevertheless, Wilfred Bion (1959) described how projective identification should be regarded as a normal as well as a pathological process. On the theme of mourning, Klein wrote:

> My experience leads me to conclude that, while it is true the characteristic of normal mourning is the individual's setting up the lost loved object inside himself, he is not doing so for the first time but, through the work of mourning, is reinstating that object as well as all his loved *internal* objects which he feels he has lost. He is therefore *recovering* what he had already attained in childhood. (Klein 1940: 362)

We have now accumulated a wide variety of theoretical positions to guide us. I will now attempt to examine the theme of psychosis in more detail, through a reading of a novel by Caribbean writer Roy Heath—*The Murderer*—which, in my opinion, makes a very significant contribution to the understanding of psychosis.

Chapter Three

A Young Man's Psychotic Breakdown

The Murderer, a novel by Roy Heath, was first published in 1978. It tells the story of the progress of a young man through a psychotic illness whom—whilst in an extremely paranoid state—commits murder.

The author is Guyanese. Guyana is a country with slavery in its history, as well as violent resistance to slavery, and a vibrant pre-slavery heritage. Indeed, Amerindians survive in the interior of the country to this day.

Guyana has a small population for its size. Large parts of the country are unfamiliar to its inhabitants, except in the form of stories and myths. The country is situated below sea-level and is subject to periodic flooding, which perhaps has a bearing on the name of the hero of Heath's novel—Galton Flood.

Heath presents a graphic account of a young man going mad, and I shall use features of the story to explore various ideas on the developmental factors which facilitate paranoia. I am interested especially in how psychotic breakdown assumes its shape, and how it is handled by the people around the person who experiences it.

* * *

Throughout the book there is a high level of aggressive hostility directed towards women. The story itself provides some clues to why this is the case. Hostility, it would seem, is the end-result of the hero's attempts (as an infant) to deal with a pathologically frustrating mother. It might be said—in addition—that an infant in this situation experiences a special type of humiliation at the hands of his first object, and that this humiliation is based in the parent's transmission to the child of a memory of slavery. It is this humiliation which gives rise to hostility.

Loitering in the background is an equally intense passion: the longing of the little boy to love freely and to be allowed to be free. If this desire was brought into the foreground it would threaten to drive the little boy—and the grown man—to madness. In the novel it is repeatedly suggested that—during times of breakdown—stabilisation can be achieved through the caring of men for other men. Even so, the paranoia from which Galton suffers is not simply a defence against homosexuality—as Freud would argue, along the lines suggested in his paper on Daniel Paul Schreber and paranoia (Freud 1911). I think that—on one level, at least—it has more to do with Galton defending himself from his own hostile feelings. On another level, he can be seen as searching for a bearer of tenderness who does not threaten to 'flood' him. In Galton's mind, it is his father who presents this possibility, rather than his mother.

We learn a great deal about Galton in the first few pages of the novel. A consideration of Galton's 'internal world' must involve exploration of what goes on around him, because so much of himself appears to be projected onto others and onto his surroundings. Galton's story is ordinary, painful, and also—at times—chilling, yet assuaged by some humorous touches. It is the story of someone who is unable to attain object-love, and who eventually comes to realise that this is the case. His experience of grief, which arises from a sense of frustration, scorn, and humiliation, is so terrible that it turns to persecution.

The author introduces us to the family. Firstly we encounter Galton, then his mother, then his brother Selwyn, and finally his father. Mr. Flood is presented (to borrow a term coined by Schreber) as 'unmanned'. At first it seems he is this way due to the behaviour of his wife. However, even outside the home, it seems he is comfortable adopting a more feminine and maternal role:

> ...the incident that Galton recalled most clearly as being associated with that visit concerned an infant, who had been creeping naked about the house. The child messed on the floor, and the host promptly called his wife to wipe up the filth. Galton's father, having placed his hand of cards face down on the table, picked up the child and addressed it with terms of endearment. (p. 5-6)[11]

This might be read as a distorted memory belonging to Galton, of being held by his father.

At the beginning of the story Galton is nineteen-years-old, and has started working in his brother's shop. His father has died, and he has just made friends with a young man called Winston, who has a girlfriend. Before the end of the chapter, however, his mother also dies, within a year of his father's death. Even though she is dead, Galton wants to get away from a mother by whom he still feels mocked, flooded, humiliated and controlled (p. 7-8).

Our attention is drawn early on towards the conflicting influences of good and evil—situated in the external environment—namely, the church Galton is obliged to attend, and the salacious dancing of a neighbour. Galton's conflict, whilst watching the neighbour, is expressed in terms of—on the one hand—his inability to 'keep his eyes off the folds of dry skin trembling between the rows of glistening sequins' (p. 4) and—on the other—his disgust at the neighbour's gestures, and his perception of her (rather than of himself) as lecherous. We are informed that Galton himself cannot dance, although he wishes he could (p. 7). He has internalised an idea of his mother's: that dancing is sinful unless the dancers are married, because dancing is like engaging in public love-making (p. 8).

Already then, at this point in the novel, the external constraints on Galton are stripped away, and his personality and its internal conflict are laid bare. We also learn that Galton both admires and envies his only sibling, Selwyn, a brother who 'generally displayed a degree of independence reserved for husbands of adoring wives' (p. 3).

Overall, this is a picture of a young man totally unprepared for adulthood. We are told that there is 'a suitable period' of mourning after Mrs. Flood's death (p. 7)—but not, significantly, that she herself was mourned. Afterwards, Galton attempts to pay a visit to the dance hall. However, before entering he is 'seized by a sort of panic' (p. 7) and turns tail. As a consequence, it seems, he feels driven to leave the family home. He receives no sympathy from his brother, whose earlier response to his difficulties—perhaps in identification with their mother—was mockery: 'he ought to study for the ministry' (p. 4). Galton, in order to escape further humiliation from soon-to-be-married Selwyn, begins an journey which will take him into psychosis. He sets out for an area of the country known as 'the interior'. He takes some of his inheritance with him—emotional and well as financial—to this place far removed from social niceties, and definitely far away from women.

On the way, Galton arrives at a town called Linden where he lodges with a Mr. Burrowes and his daughter, Gemma. Her mother died when she was five, and her father brought her up. Galton discovers in himself a passion for Gemma. However, unknown to Galton—because she keeps the fact a secret— Gemma is already the mother of a child. What occurs between her and Galton can hardly be called 'falling in love', and is short-lived. Galton is as inhibited as ever, but seems calmer during this stage of his journey than at its beginning. Yet the moment he demonstrates his love for Gemma by kissing her, he finds himself struggling to cope with an opposing feeling; he is foundering in a swell of jealousy (p. 20). There is a third-party with whom Galton must contend; an 'Oedipal situation' would be one way of describing this. The third-party is a young man Galton observes with Gemma, 'who stood in front of her, enter- taining her with his talk' (p. 19). Galton succeeds in triumphing over this rival, but is soon having to cope with newly disturbed feelings. At Linden he encounters a character known as 'the Walk-Man'—a man who claims to be able to read a person's character from the way they walk, but who is also referred to by his detractors as 'the Lie-Man' (p. 21). The trigger for the destruction of Galton's attempt to love Gemma is neither the Oedipal rival, nor the trouble-making Walk-Man, but the moment in which he mistakes the Walk-Man's wife for his mother:

> Galton followed him into the drawing room, where the wife was sitting on the far side, her back to the door.
> 'So you come home after all,' she said, half turning, so that Galton only saw her profile in the half-light.
> 'God!' he exclaimed, gaping at the Walk-Man's wife.

'What's the matter?' asked the Walk-Man, alarmed at Galton's expression.

His wife got up and came towards them and Galton, on seeing her more closely said 'I'm sorry. It's just that—in the dark and seeing you like that... you looked like my mother.'

'That's all!' said the Walk-Man. 'I thought you were going to have a fit... My wife Mabel.' (p. 23-4)

Soon afterwards she makes Galton a sour drink (p. 26).

It is a natural part of the process of mourning to believe one sees the person who has died or to mistake others for them. However, this incident also suggests that Galton's difficulties are not Oedipal—in the classical, Freudian sense—but are entirely pre-Oedipal.

Heath writes:

All the happiness he [Galton] had accumulated these last few weeks was erased with the few words spoken by someone who evidently bore Burrowes a grudge. Yet, even if the Walk-Man had lied he could not live in that house any longer than was necessary. (p. 27)

The offending 'few words' spoken by the Walk-Man are: '*she won't marry you*' (p. 25). However, these words simply feed an already well-established paranoid delusion system in Galton, as is evidenced by a later comment made by Selwyn on Galton's ongoing suspicious nature (p. 44). Galton, it seems, wants to revenge himself upon his mother by punishing Gemma, through abandoning her. When she responds in a way that makes it clear to Galton she is a separate person, with her own mind—saying: 'You don't have to run from me' (p. 29)—he has his first major crisis. As Heath puts it, Galton is left 'stranded in some vast, unknown country, without money or resources' (p. 29):

In the dark room, hung with ancient wallpaper, now so familiar to him, an absurd idea changed his mind: he must somehow lick the wall bare of its flowers. On the cover of the book he found open on the dining table the day before she had written the quotation:

> When care draws near
> The garden of the soul lies waste

'Flowers on a partition!' he exclaimed to himself. 'Why not put manure while they're at it? Ha! Then they'd see a real garden, where rats hide and come out to devour the flowers at night.'

He began wringing his hands in great excitement and muttering to himself; and then, as if responding to some inner prompting, jumped on the bed and began licking the walls in an attempt to remove the flowers. But when his efforts proved in vain he was taken by a violent inclination to smash down the door that connected his room to Gemma's. (p. 29-30)

Galton is in no position—developmentally speaking—to take a wife. In a perverse manner he chooses to trust the lies he is told by the Walk-Man as these suit his paranoid organisation. Leaving behind the town of Linden, and Gemma, he continues on his journey to the interior. A period of two years in this region, working as a diver (symbolising, perhaps a return to the womb), and living with men who make no emotional demands upon him, helps him to stabilise himself. During this time, perhaps he was able to reach something positive deep inside himself, derived from his father. As Heath vividly portrays, however, this soon fades.

Eventually Galton returns to the parental home, carrying with him his habitual concerns and worries. He brings a caged bird as a gift for his brother, who is now married with a son and living in their parents' old house. The caged bird exactly describes Galton's own condition.

During his first night in the house, he has the following dream:

...his dead father... spoke in a way he could not understand. Then his father became John, his Amerindian friend, behind whom he was sitting in a corial. John was paddling in his unhurried style, close to the bank of a black water creek. Ahead of them was a swarm of morpho butterflies, and those that had alighted on an overhanging branch were opening and closing their wings in leisurely fashion. (p. 47-8)

On waking his first thought is that it is absurd for a man to be separate, in a room all by himself, rather than being with other men sleeping together in hammocks, keeping each other company. His next thought is 'Why do I never dream of my mother?', and then that he never wants to marry, 'not ever' (p. 48).

The dream occurs in the context of Galton being welcomed home by his brother, and finding a letter from Gemma waiting for him. She addresses Galton as her 'dear tormentor' (p. 46) and announces her desire to be with him, even if this means being part of a sadomasochistic couple. His associations to the dream—that is, the thoughts that enter his head after waking—reveal his infantile longings for closeness to a male figure who is, perhaps, merely a cover for a phallic mother, a mother with a penis. By wondering why he never dreams of his mother he is, in effect, asking 'why does she never come to me?'. In this question lies his grief at the loss of his childhood and of his mother, a loss—as yet—not consciously recognised.

Galton could not mourn his mother because he never achieved a separation from her. His father's death seems to trouble him much less than his mother's, because he idealises his father to a certain degree, and has thus attained some distance from him. The morpho butterflies he sees might be taken to represent a sexuality that lacks shape—which is, in other words, *'amorphous'*.

Galton does not take responsibility for making the decision to marry Gemma. The letter he writes in reply to her is a masterpiece of evasion (p. 55-6). He takes a lowly job as a night-watchman and hands over his responsibility for making decisions to his friend Winston. His reasons for taking this job can be variously interpreted, depending on one's theoretical position. For instance, it could be seen as a way of trying to block out 'night noises', sounds from the archaic parental couple, stimulated by the presence of an actual couple in the same house. Alternatively, he may wish to 'watch at night' in order to see if his mother will appear. I mention this because, in his culture, the spirits of the dead are expected to visit from time to time. This would be a quite normal expectation, wished-for as well as feared. The job also satisfies Galton's need for self-abasement, and to attack his brother sadistically for getting on with his own life and—as Galton would see it—for placing him in second place and ignoring him.

Galton senses a renewal of old feelings of humiliation, transferred from childhood into his present situation. He believes these feelings arise from outside; that they are not of his own making but are put into him, no longer by his mother, but by his brother and by Nekka, his sister-in-law. He conceives an especially intense hatred towards Nekka. These feelings make him want to effect a hostile separation from them. The next minute, however, he is more content: 'I am very happy living with my brother and sister-in-law' (p. 55). Yet in the same breath he projects his own mad feelings onto the big family with seven girls that lives next door: 'They are all mad!' (p. 55).

Eventually Galton realises that his sister-in-law is not happy with his presence. He moves out of Selwyn's house and into that of his friend Winston, with its leaky roof. It is at this point that Galton marries Gemma, and takes her to live with him at Winston's, apparently in the hope that he might finally obtain what he needs from the close presence of both his wife and his friend. Unfortunately, the situation quickly breaks down. Galton perceives Selwyn as distant and neglectful, and it is not long before he begins to feel persecuted by feelings of jealousy and envy—particularly concerning 'this household of three generations' (p. 73) which comprises Winston, and Winston's wife, daughter, and mother-in-law.

For the first time in his life Galton starts drinking. Soon, driven by hostility, he moves himself and his wife out into further degrading circumstances. The seedy place in which he chooses to live, in the wharf area, on the edge of the land, represents an internal transition to a state in which Galton is metaphorically 'on the edge'. He strikes up a friendship with a homosexual neighbour—a police informant—and seems utterly bent upon creating a situation of maximum humiliation for Gemma, as well as for himself. He expects that she will desert him, yet she remains loyal to her husband. Even so, gaining a little awareness of his own paranoid state seems merely to redouble his anger. Heath tells us: 'Sometimes his heart was so filled with such murderous hatred towards women he dreaded the long hours by his wife's side' (p. 114).

Gemma, adopting the role of victim to Galton, her 'tormentor', fails to recognise the reality of her situation, that 'the essential term of marriage [for him] ...could only be the complete subservience of the woman' (p. 129). She thinks that she might be pregnant (p. 127), and makes one feeble attempt to have someone rescue her—the man by whom she had her child (p. 125-6). Here—as elsewhere in the novel—the message seems to be that only men can be called upon for rescue; women are absent. I am not in a position to link this directly with the author's own life, but it seems fair to say that we are all linked in some way to our creations.

Galton sinks further and further into paranoia, helped along by the malice of his friend and neighbour, the informant. Galton recognises that there is something wrong with himself, but seems to be on a course towards destruction from which he will not be diverted. He believes it is his marriage that makes him ill, yet he confesses to Gemma: 'It's not the noises [from outside] that wake me... I don't know. I only know it's not the noises... If we don't separate...' (p. 126). She accepts his wish that they should part yet, by doing this, provokes him to outrage at her capacity to exist as a separate being away from him. It would seem his mother's death was a similar outrage, leaving him unprepared for life as an adult.

All his old anxieties concerning separation from his mother resurface at this point, together with revengeful wishes. The impossibility of attaining an intimate relationship, combined with the unbearability of not attaining one, leads him into another crisis. He begins to feel haunted by a belief that his mother's body was not buried (p. 128). It is in this highly disturbed state that he finally murders his wife (p. 131).

Afterwards, dejectedly, he declares: '*I* can't share, you see... My generosity isn't real; it's only skin deep' (p. 137). He *knows* he cannot love. Immediately after Gemma's murder, it is the company of men which helps him regain a measure of composure, but which does not last. His terror increases, and he fears further torment. He justifies his actions on the grounds that Gemma 'wasn't fit to live' (p. 220)—a not unusual justification, among a certain type of murderer (Hyatt Williams 1960). His persecutory feelings worsen: 'The trouble is they never buried my mother,' he insists, 'but she doesn't persecute him' (p. 223), meaning Selwyn. He has the sensation of being in a bottle, which must be kept uncovered if he is to stay alive (p. 213). This represents a complete regression of the infant back into the mother's body. That the bottle must be kept open to ensure survival is interesting: it allows for visitors, perhaps his father. Indeed, Galton chooses to allow his brother, now a good father, husband, and owner of a pharmacy—a place with bottles—to take responsibility for his permanent care, outside of an institution.

Chapter Four

The Psychoanalysis of Galton Flood

Galton is the opposite of his brother Selwyn. Galton is physically taller, but his development is stunted in every other way (p. 3). Heath presents Galton as lacking freedom, self-assurance, and a sense of feeling loved. Galton feels trapped and stifled by the influence of a mother with many fears, who displays a tendency to split her world into good and bad. She exercises strict control over her child's contact with his father and the outside world, and his father colludes in this. There is very little of the father in Galton's life, and even when his father is present he seems a somewhat reduced figure:

> Galton remembered the father of his childhood as a jovial man who in later years fell silent whenever he came home at night. His heroic efforts to avoid quarrelling with his wife were not always successful. (p. 4)

This process of wearing down and reducing the father must have taken years, and in the meantime the two brothers would have had very different experiences of their parents. This could account—in part—for the different ways in which they developed.

Selwyn seems to have enjoyed a more available father and, perhaps, a happier mother, and to have internalised good parental objects, whereas Galton seems to have had much less of a father and thus less to internalise. Galton's need to seek out men to support him suggests an ongoing attempt to fill this gap within himself. He needs support to maintain his masculinity. When, in late adolescence, he is hit by two bereavements—particularly by the death of his mother—his hostility is fully exposed: 'Galton developed such hostile feelings towards the house he shared with his brother that he announced his intention of going away' (p. 8). These feelings were the end-product of years of frustration, humiliation, fear, envy, shame and grief.

It would be easy to slot Galton into any of the current psychoanalytic theoretical structures, but without paying attention to the historical, social and cultural context against which this character emerges. Slavery forms a big part of this historical background, and impacts significantly upon the personal, even though slavery ended more than a hundred years ago and even though culture is always rapidly changing. Some things, however, have not changed all that much. *Fear*—for example—which was instilled into males in particular during slavery and its aftermath, has had an enduring impact on interpersonal relations because it has been internalised and, consequently, has contributed to high levels of castration anxiety. The influence of this has been hugely underestimated. Only when this is overcome will men and women take their rightful places *alongside* one another. Until this happens, bonding between men and women remains problematic.

The twentieth century delivered radical movements which have helped to deal with these problems. These movements have been extremely valuable, as there remains much work to be done at a political level. However, I believe that many of the problems which require attention are just as much 'internal' as they are 'external'. For instance, in Heath's novel we encounter Galton's father, who cannot (or will not) help extricate his son from the clutches of the mother. Yet it is vitally important that fathers—or someone carrying out the father-function—takes on this task. It is necessary because women from this background carry a tendency to hate men, rooted in times of slavery during which men failed to protect them. A father who releases his son from the clutches of the mother, however, is then forced into retaking his place alongside his wife and becoming part of a three-some. The requirement to share his wife may present difficulties which are not only Oedipal, but which are also rooted in a tendency to view women as disloyal—again, this belongs to the context of slavery. Consequently it can be seen how, in the environment of distrust which slavery created, children are used to regulate the distance between parents. Galton Flood is the depiction of a child who has been used in this way.

In *The Murderer* Heath depicts an external world in which a culture of perversion and sadism has been imposed upon the people—for this is what slavery amounts to. People were forced to witness extremes of cruelty and terror. They had fear and shame instilled in them for the precise purpose of exercising control over their lives. What would be surprising was if this were *not* passed down to the present population.

Within the context of slavery, some women and old men were able to appropriate a small degree of power. Women were raped, but could also seduce the slave-master, produce children, and thus enrich the plantation and its owner. Women also had the power to kill their new-born children, and thus to reduce the production of new lives and—therefore—wealth.

Meanwhile, African men who were made into slaves were humiliated into sharing African women with European men in positions of power over them. Furthermore, the men were also forced to raise the children of these unions, even whilst both woman and child remained the property of the slave-owner (D'Aguiar 1995). Older men might find it easier to accept their fate, and sometimes lived out their days keeping the younger men in line, in return for a certain amount of benevolence from the slave-master.

Over hundreds of years, then, slavery reduced both men and women. However, it reduced men *more* than women. The women who have emerged from the background of these conditions know their potential for power, although they are often afraid to make use of it. They know their history without having to hear it told to them; they know what happened to their men and to their children. The men—meanwhile—know the power of the women and fear to challenge it, even to this day, and despite its tenuous quality.

Obviously, over time, many men in many families have regained respect. They have authority and are able to share it with women. It is the way in which male children have been parented which has had a lot to do with this recovery. Unfortunately, however, in many other families respect for males is a lost cause. In these cases, male children are more likely to suffer severe castration anxiety. Sometimes the father-function is assumed by another family member—often a senior female—or sometimes it is simply not assumed by anyone. (I am referring here not only to nuclear family structures, but to any of the various family structures to be found in the Caribbean.) We sense how Mr. Flood, Galton's father, brought his own castration fears into his marriage, and how both he and his wife succeeded in passing these on to their second son. Mrs. Flood, for her part, brought her scorn of males into the marriage, passing this on to both her husband and Galton. However, she had no hold over her first-born Selwyn, who represents the real man in the household and the personification of freedom from slavery.

Although it seems she was in total control of Galton, Heath informs us that she herself never actually felt certain this was the case: 'his mother's hold over him, uncertain in her eyes but very real to Galton, kept him by her side' (p. 6). This perhaps explains the intensity of her need to be so controlling—as an attempt to *make sure* Galton is under her power—and might be read as a reflection of the slave-owner's feelings. Galton, however, felt himself totally controlled and totally without the means to put an end to the situation.

However, his mother's injunctions could only have stuck if they encountered something within Galton on which they could stick. We are shown how, as he reaches late adolescence, Galton seeks out the company of his friend Winston, in order to firm up his masculinity (p. 7). Galton must, at times, have been forced to wonder whether he was a girl or a boy because—in his society— traditionally it is boys who are allowed out of the house, and girls who are more likely to be kept inside 'to help their mother'.

From the very beginning of the novel Galton's relations with his object appear to be very disturbed:

> He himself dared not cultivate an affection lest it reared up and attacked him; nor could he express his dislike for a person for fear that the intensity of his disapproval might seem absurd, and with time he brushed aside every

impulse to display any tender emotion towards the members of his family. (p. 6)

It seems likely Galton experienced very little tenderness during his childhood—whether or not it was actually offered to him—and, as a consequence, he is unable to show it towards his nearest and dearest.

One of the earliest scenes from Galton's childhood depicted by Heath concerns a memory of his father holding a small baby which messes itself (p. 5-6). The situation described, then, concerns a baby receiving tenderness from a male who is not the infant's father. This may well have been the situation of Galton as an infant: feeling himself in a mess from which his father fails to lift him, whilst wishing for his father to do so. What we do know for certain is that at the age of three—by which time he has language—Galton witnesses his mother 'belabouring his father in a frenzy of anger' (p. 102). If she is so powerful that she can subdue the father, a grown man, then she must also be able to do the same to Galton, a small boy. In symbolic terms, she is able to castrate both father and son. What is a child to make of his mother flaring up into what seems like a murderous rage, and of his father seemingly not available to rescue him from her? He may have feared taking his father's side—as part of the normal way of growing up and away from mother—in case she rejected him for his disloyalty. But then how could he have persuaded himself in the first place to take sides with a weak man? Mother—a woman—must have seemed the parent with all the power.

The defeat of his father instils in Galton a feeling of wanting 'the world to come to an end' (p. 102). This remains with him, and would have hindered his Oedipal struggles. We are told that his father is a gambler, and that his gambling worries his wife. We do not know for sure whether his gambling and her anger are connected, but we might presume that they are, and that there is disturbance to their sexual relationship, given the way he finds his excitement outside the home and she is unable to turn her attention away from her son.

Mother tells her son:

'Your father is a gambler, Galton. He's steeped in sin and shame and God's mercy is turned away from this house. Kneel down and pray for your father and beg God to spare us and to remember that he was not always like that.' (p. 171)

The nature of the burden that this little boy is asked to carry—from the age of three—is sin, shame, and fear. In addition he is being asked to help make his father better ('like he used to be') for his mother's benefit. This is a task at which he is bound to fail and which consequently, over time, sharpens his avoidance of competition. However, putting all this aside, mother is at least acknowledging that there is something wrong in the family. The quarrelling wife may be viewed as trying to ensure worries are listened to and sorted out. Nevertheless, instilling fear in another person simply provokes avoidance.

Galton grows up in a world in which there is a clear division of people into saints and sinners—saintly mother, and sinning father. As a result, the mechanism of projecting unwanted parts of the self into others (parts of mother into father) is already well-established as part of his mental structure, if he chooses to adopt it. Indeed he does, and in due course becomes paranoid. Galton feels *entitled* to be hostile, because—as he sees things— he is persecuted. However, he has no means at his disposal to ascertain whether his persecution originates from inside or outside himself. Some externally persecutory environments are more conducive to paranoia than others, and Galton's was certainly one of these.

Theoretical perspectives on Galton's development

Freud's theory of progression through developmental stages and phases suggests that Galton has difficulties situated in the early oral phase of his psychosexual development. He cannot let go of his mother and separate from her. He also displays signs of anal-sadistic fixation. Most little boys love their mothers faithfully—as can be seen in Freud's 'Little Hans' case study (Freud 1909)—but Galton's love for his mother is spoiled.

If one employs a 'deficit model' of psychoanalysis, then the mother could be held responsible for pulling him further and further into a partnership with her against father. Father could also be regarded as contributing to his son's difficulties, because of his commitment to avoidance of conflict, which simply serves to push Galton further away from him. These conditions are apt to produce high levels of hostility towards the parents—towards mother in particular. In Freudian terms, this would prevent progression through the Oedipus complex.

It is significant that Galton cannot allow himself to see his wife's genitals (p. 91). Seeing them would have increased his anxieties. If she were seen by him to be castrated, then the possibility of his own castration becomes very real—it could be his turn next! On the other hand, if she were seen by him to have a penis, then he might feel driven to eliminate her. At the height of his psychotic breakdown he is stuck in a similarly sadistic state which—in response to being asked whether he admits to killing his wife—prompts him to reply: 'You don't understand. I don't admit it. I *proclaim* it' (p. 220).

In Lacanian terms, the two conditions which work together and which are necessary to bring about psychosis are already present in Galton's childhood. The child is the object of his mother's desire, and she is unable to turn her desire to his father. Consequently, the father is not internally symbolised for Galton; he erases the father and, in doing so, discounts reality. This situation leaves behind a hole which becomes filled with hallucinations and delusions.

In terms of Kleinian object relations, Galton's anxieties as a young man are, in fact, very old. They are located in the Kleinian paranoid-schizoid position. Galton can be understood as having been an intensely anxious infant and child, persecuted by anxiety. Because of his destructiveness, he was unable to maintain a good internal object and to move into the Kleinian depressive position, and from there to the beginnings of the Oedipus complex. He is certainly inhibited from doing what most children do—that is, gradually separating from their

mothers and going out to play with other children, as his brother Selwyn did during his childhood (p. 3-4). Galton, instead, is
inclined to keep his good and bad parts very widely apart from
each other, and to experience the outside world away from
mother as *all* bad, as a dangerous place which should be avoided. Indeed, from the very first chapter of the novel there is evidence that Galton is terrified of going into the outside world (p.
8). When he finally does so, it is in a spirit of turning away from
mother *with hostility*. As Klein suggests, this fear of separation is
connected to the infant and child's feelings of intense sadism
towards the mother (Klein 1946: 13-4; 1952: 92), and there is
abundant evidence of these in Galton as the story reaches its cli-
max.

To make use of another object relations theorist, Winnicott,
who also employs a 'deficit model', leads to a conclusion that
the baby Galton and his mother are unable to lead separate exis-
tences on account of a refusal of the father (for whatever reason)
to insert himself between them. Without a separate existence
there is no opportunity for the infant Galton to build a true self,
to have his own mind and his own body. Instead, he erects a
false self which fits in with his mother's wishes, but which also
makes him vulnerable to psychosis.

Employing this theoretical approach, one uncovers a mother
exercising her power over her son by way of scornfulness and
bullying. He is broken by shame, for example, by the way his
mother handles a potential rival for his love:

> One day when a girl from his school came to call for him
> his mother laughed as if it were a big joke; Galton
> remained inside, his eyes closed tight in shame. (p. 3)

We are told that he sustains many more humiliations at his
mother's hands. The effect was for him to begin treating himself
as an object of debasement:

> Thus he frequently saw himself driving a dray cart
> through streets lined with his relations and acquain-

tances, who were pointing in his direction each with their mouth covered with one hand. (p. 6)

Galton's energy is taken up with repressing enormous feelings of hatred towards his mother, and with denying these feelings. His problems, therefore, seem to focus more upon a mother-complex than upon anything else. His hate arises partly out of the frustration of never being able to work through the real world of the Oedipus complex and to resolve it satisfactorily. He wants his mother but cannot have his mother, and he hates her for this.

For me, another important reason which accounts for the unhappy state of Galton's family is the absence of grandparents. The function of grandparents is multi-dimensional: they can act as regulators of distance between couples and between parents and children. They can offer additional parental care to the grandchild, and thus increase the solidity of his or her development. They can also offer parenting to the parents themselves. However, there is no hint of an extended family network in the Flood household. It is conceivable that the grandparents might be dead, and that their deaths are still hanging over the family, causing grief which has to be defended against. This was indeed the situation for Africans made slaves in the Caribbean; their parents—whom they left behind—might just as well have been dead. Galton is himself aware of feeling particularly envious of Winston's three generational household, just before he takes flight from their home (p. 73). The child in this household—whom he seems particularly to dislike—has a grandparent. We are also told how Galton, at the age of five or six, was separated for three weeks from his mother whilst she was ill (p. 212). This necessitated him to stay not in the care of a grandparent, at home, but apparently alone, with a distant relative in the country. Furthermore, at this age he became consciously acquainted with death, when he saw coffins in a funeral parlour (p. 102). Funeral processions are not mentioned, but it is unlikely that these could have escaped his attention at that age.

Fun never comes for free in this little boy's life—or so he is led to believe. It comes through stealing it, or paying for it—

through a ride on the dray cart, or by a picture of a star in return for a kiss from the girl next door (p. 102).

Of the many themes which run through the novel, I shall now concentrate on three: separation anxiety, grief and longing, and imprisonment.

Separation anxiety

It seems to me very likely that a little boy like Galton would fill up his mind with sexual matters. Consider: there he is, tied to his mother, meeting her own narcissistic needs. There is no suggestion of the presence of an active father, but only of a man beaten down by his wife, and barely trusted to function as a father towards her most precious possession. All Galton's energies are taken up with this state of affairs, making it impossible for him to escape and join his peers at play. His education may also have suffered as a result.

As I have mentioned, receiving a kiss from a girl is not an easy matter for Galton. His thought that he is not going to marry—not ever—is the impulse of a little boy who is already engaged to his mother. Consequently he grows into a young man with complicated fantasies about women's bodies, apparent in his insistence that Gemma keeps on her underwear during intimacies (p. 91). He has no wish to see her genitals, for fear—perhaps—of what he might discover there. This combination of (at some level) feeling like an object of seduction, feeling excited and yet at the same time consciously aware of sin, and feeling prevented from venturing out to find little women of his own (seven young girls lived right next door [p. 56]) creates something explosive in Galton. His mother has to die before he can even begin to see and feel for himself that he has a problem when it comes to being a separate being, which is a necessary condition for truly 'falling in love'.

The theme of separation anxiety is illustrated further in the way Galton deals with two subsequent crises. Firstly, in the way he initiates an abandonment of Gemma in Linden when she turns bad in his mind—that is, when she becomes to him a person who wants to trap him. Her response—'you don't have to run from me'—makes him feel the full force of her separateness, and he becomes psychotic (p. 29-30). Even though it is he who initiates the break, he feels it is she who has abandoned him.

The second crisis, also initiated by him, which carries right through to the murder of Gemma and beyond, seems to begin the moment he finds himself sexually aroused by the informant's mother, a woman in her fifties (p. 111-2). Gemma's response—'there are women like that, Galton' (p. 112)—throws him into furious denial. He cannot bear the idea that he is a man 'like that'. This is followed by a violent admission to Gemma which frightens her: 'I should've done it, since I was a boy,' he says, 'snuffed this thing out before it grew fat' (p. 113). He is talking about his mother-complex.

The word that comes into Galton's mind during his descent into the hell of psychotic breakdown is 'independent' (p. 128-9). 'She wanted her independence', he declares. 'I gave her it' (p. 163). However, independence is the very thing he cannot give himself. Some deficit theorists would argue that Galton has not been parented in a way which could enable him to be independent. He does not know how to be a separate being. To him, it is an outrage to discover Gemma's difference from himself, and for this she must be snuffed out.

The murder he commits is not simply stored-up vengeance. Galton has delusions of persecution; he thinks his marriage is making him ill, and that Gemma does not love him as she once did, and thus that *she* has put murderous thoughts into him (p. 128-9). He also thinks that this mother's body is not buried (p. 128), although a part of him realises that he is ill (p. 173). He kills his wife, then, in order to relieve himself of feelings of persecution. He is attempting to rid himself not only of his wife, but also of the depressed and phallic mother who has taken over his mind, and who makes him feel inadequate. The goodness from his father—which he appears to recapture during his journey to the Interior—does not seem solid enough to withstand his hate, and it becomes lost. Galton is unable to turn to his brother or to his friend for help. It is to strangers, often men without names (such as the character known to us only as 'the watchman') that he turns. Towards these men he feels a sense of superiority, and a confidence that they will make no emotional demands on him.

In object relations terminology, Galton's relationship with Gemma is not—in any case—a relationship with a whole object. Heath suggests that the passion which arises in him soon after meeting her is simply 'a release from all the constraints of years gone by' (p. 16). She is not a whole person, then, but merely a functionary, a part-object. Galton shows signs of omnipotence— that is, of wishing to keep control over her just as the baby wishes to control the mother's breast. However, Galton could not be weaned and encouraged to move on towards separation in a positive way, allowing his object to become human, someone real and with feelings. He cannot allow himself to experience her separateness and her absence, as this would mean coming into contact with the reality of unbearable grief of many years' standing. The psychic foundations for building the house that Gemma wants are entirely lacking. Instead, he attacks her in a sadistic way. His destruction of his internal object expresses itself externally in a psychosis, during which he commits murder. His mind disintegrates totally, and he can only stabilise it by crawling inside his delusional 'bottle' (p. 213), whilst insisting that the bottle be left open. In this way he restores a link with both parents. He becomes a baby who cries for all the world to hear.

Grief and longing

The theme of grief and longing is connected to separation anxiety and to imprisonment. As we have seen, there is a strong sense in the novel of the absence of grandparents, and of a lively, well-functioning parental couple. The grief which this causes is repressed in the generation above Galton, as well as by Galton himself, but it is this repression which causes so much trouble.

By the age of three, Galton knows that his parents are unhappy. He wonders why they are fighting, why his father is so subdued at home, and why his mother should be so quarrelsome. They are presented as a profoundly isolated couple. Galton grieves for his unhappy parents who cannot or will not be fixed, no matter how much he submits to their wishes. His mother's wish seems to be to keep him by her side, and his father's is that Galton should keep his mother company, in order to leave his father free to go out with his friends. Galton's longing is for the absent male object of his dream (p. 47-8). The swarm of morpho butterflies in the dream, which could be taken to represent sexual (bad) thoughts, are outside, are away from the couple who sail along close together on untroubled waters. It is the movement of the butterflies' wings which brings the dream to the end—and perhaps this is the movement of Galton's thoughts themselves, towards sexual intercourse. It should be remembered that John the Amerindian, who features in the dream, is a provider of food and a caretaker and that, on waking, Galton's grief for his mother is poignantly sharp.

Imprisonment

The novel presents a picture of a child imprisoned by conflict expressed in his external world, and then expressed in his internal world by a feeling of imprisonment by his mother. Separating from a hated object is no easy matter, for it is uncertain whether the hated object can survive attacks made on it. Consequently, Galton has to remain near his mother in order to keep an eye on her, to make sure that she stays alive. We see this, for instance, in the way that Heath tells us how Galton, as a child, was not encouraged to play outside with friends (p. 3). However, it seems that Galton himself has no desire to run out and play, like other children. He is a child deserted by his father and—over time—also by his brother, yet he is not in touch with feeling deserted. His feeling of imprisonment is captured in his consequent idea that 'life is one long hell' (p. 173).

Mrs. Flood, in all likelihood, feels imprisoned too. We glean this from the words Heath gives to Gemma in her reply to Galton's letter: 'You men lock women up in small places and expect them to be normal' (p. 57). Mrs. Flood is imprisoned by her own conflicts, and so proceeds to imprison her younger son, to press him into her service, like a kind of slave. Her son's role is to help her in the absence of her husband's ability to help. She seems convinced that her unhappiness is caused by her husband—which may not, in fact, be the case.

While Galton serves as a regulator of distance between his parents, his mother can keep dirty sex (that is, sex which is not for the procreation of children) at bay. Her moral superiority is sustained by religion, which supplies a direct line to the Almighty. Mr. Flood's gambling, meanwhile, can be viewed from his point of view as a form of anti-depressant.

Galton's crises are all associated with feelings of imprisonment. One instance that comes to mind is his response to Gemma's suggestion that they save for a home of their own. The thought of it makes him feel so trapped that he resists by moving out from Winston's at once (p. 90).

* * *

Had Galton lived in a society in which psychiatrists were plentiful, it seems very likely that he would have been diagnosed as suffering from paranoid schizophrenia. However, Mrs. Flood herself feels that there is simply something bad hanging over her house—'God's mercy is turned away from this house' (p. 171)—although she is not clear what this might be. I would suggest that this is the unconscious knowledge of slavery and its aftermath (that is, the inability to talk about things in a personal way), which creates a special kind of anxiety that manifests itself in various forms. It seems to me that slavery looms over the characters like one big castration threat, and determines their ability to form couples. Everyone has to deal with the anxieties of the Oedipus complex, but these are made more complicated by the reality of a violent past.

The character Walk-Man, we are told, is a descendent of Cuffy, leader of a slave rebellion (p. 21). However it is the Walk-Man's lies to which Galton chooses to listen, rather than to his truths—even though the Walk-Man confesses that he is a liar (p. 32). This could be taken as a hint of an underlying concern with the truth and lies about slavery—about who was responsible for it in the first place. Was it a particular group of people, or is the responsibility for it shared?

The answer to this question takes the form of the way in which the castration complex is resolved, and in each case the answer is acted out through the family. For instance, the father of the family seems to have submitted internally to castration anxiety. He is rather like the men who submitted to violence from their owners, who lost their manhood and were transformed into what they must have felt to be nothing better than women. Bullying and being bullied were thus internalised as a result of slavery. Alongside this are the effects of a knowledge that people act the way they do in the present because they were driven crazy in the past. Allowance is made for madness in a society which has experienced slavery, and is tolerated in a way one does not encounter elsewhere. Men know—inside themselves—of a time when they could do nothing to help their women. This knowledge paralyses them.

To have a bullying wife, like Mrs. Flood, presents a husband like Mr. Flood with an enormous amount of anxiety, against which he must defend himself. His search for prototypes of this situation leads him back to his mother—who more than likely bullied him also—and, in addition, to archaic bullies such as ancestors and slave-owners. During slavery people's bodies were violated—male as well as female. This process spread terror, which resulted in castration fear becoming *conscious* fear. Furthermore, the greatest trauma for men made slaves was that through the sexual act they themselves became implicated as abusers, by producing children which became other people's possessions. In this way, men felt robbed in a fundamental sense, and—at the same time—they felt *part of* the system which abused their women. The men, therefore, were placed in a quite impossible situation, in which they felt like abusers whilst being abused themselves.

Over time, many Africans in the Caribbean recovered sufficiently to stand up to their persecutors, and to play their part in the abolition of slavery. Nevertheless, for a man to assert himself and to gain respect in his family—even whilst respecting his wife and children—is to be riddled with anxiety, conscious or unconscious, of being identified or identifying with the slave-owner. It should be remembered, meanwhile, that women in plantation societies, by tradition, had to manage without men as protectors. Some women became violent as a result of this process, and this violence is evident in Mrs. Flood.

For some men the castration threat is so frightening that different strategies are found to defend against the fear, although they all cluster around the basic mechanism of 'avoidance'. For instance, agency workers are well acquainted with the strategy termed 'non-attendance'. Another way out of the anxiety is homosexual fantasy, as a means of avoiding pain. In this fantasy—as in Galton's dream—the man has a peaceful relationship with another man, in which nothing at all is created for the slave-master. Consequently, there will be no further possibility of having to share or lose a precious possession—a child—or to be scorned and humiliated. Galton and his father might have shared precisely such a fantasy. Another escape from anxiety is to take the fantasy further into a homosexual relationship. Yet another possibility is a particular kind of inter-racial union in which members of the couple adopt complementary dominant and subordinate roles. In each of these alternatives the castration threat becomes less terrifying, and with less fear the conflict can then be negotiated. Feeling less fear enables both men and women to take their rightful places alongside one another.

Mr. Flood neither stages an insurrection against Mrs. Flood (as a woman who holds power, who has replaced the slave-owner)nor does he assert his right as a parent—more particularly, a parent of a male child. He is, I suspect, far too anxious to do either, and so goes into avoidance, spending his time with male friends outside the home.

Mrs. Flood contributes to the circularity of the problem which confronts males by bringing up Galton tightly by her side, almost as if he were a daughter. She may well have wanted their second child to be a daughter, which would explain why Selwyn escapes through a different resolution to the problem. Whereas Mr. Flood avoids dealing with his own violent feelings about the situation, his younger son ends up dealing with it twice over—for both of them.

* * *

What I wish to suggest is specific to the patient or client of Caribbean background are particular anxieties —for men and women—which are associated with non-resolution of the Oedipus complex. These unresolved, very old anxieties find their way into the next generation through parenting.

Cultures which have experienced slavery possess a memory of men being useless. By 'men' I mean more than just father, husband, brother—but instead *all males in general*. Consequently, if men are so useless, why bother to include them in families? Because of this strong internalisation, which is a direct result of slavery, it is harder to bring up boys to reach their full potential without an active and helpful father-presence. Many mothers do not themselves have internal 'good-enough fathers' to bring to their care of their sons. However it will also be seen, in some of the case studies which follow, that girls are also troubled by the absence of the father.

The consequences of the passage through slavery are not all negative—as Selwyn, the personification of freedom, is there for us to see. But slavery has left its scars, as evidenced by the themes in the novel which I chose to highlight. The novel leaves in the reader an overwhelming impression of wishing to escape, in both the physical and psychical sense. This wish amounts to 'avoidance' which was, after all, a useful survival strategy during slavery times. The most positive aspect of the experience of slavery is the knowledge of freedom, which would not be so available to the mind if its opposite were not so thoroughly understood. From feeling this thing called 'freedom' comes the possibility of an optimistic approach to living, regardless of setbacks.

PART TWO

The Case Histories

Chapter Five

On a Male Baby's Earliest Vicissitudes

Much of Galton Flood's fictional babyhood is not made available to us. However, in this chapter I shall present more detailed observations on what passes between a young male baby and his parents—in particular his mother—by referring to actual case material. I hope to demonstrate the ways in which the child sometimes learns *fear* from his parents, and the ways in which this makes it difficult for him to resolve the Oedipus complex.

* * *

Baby G was born in the United Kingdom. His mother emigrated to the UK when she was eleven-years-old, in order to rejoin her mother after some years of separation. During this time Baby G's mother had been cared for by a maternal aunt and grandmother. My understanding of the situation is that there were no men actively involved in her care, and that Baby G's grandmother had migrated to the UK entirely on her own.

Baby G's mother became pregnant for the first time during her teens. The father of this first child wanted to marry her. She refused this offer and eventually he married another woman, but he maintained an interest in their child, Baby G's half-brother. He also provided some voluntary financial support, and their son went to him for regular weekend visits.

Baby G's father—meanwhile—was born in the UK of Caribbean parents. At the age of seven his parents returned to the Caribbean and took him with them—to the same country from which Baby G's mother originated. On reaching adulthood Baby G's father left his parents' home and came back alone to the UK, where he began his relationship with Baby G's mother.

Unlike Baby G's mother, his father had grown up with a mother *and* a father present throughout his life, and his parents seem to have co-operated well in taking care of him. He and Baby G's mother first had a daughter, and then—finally—Baby G himself was born, his mother's third child.

I first met Baby G's mother a week before his birth. His father was abroad at the time, visiting his parents, and news of the birth was sent out to him. He did not return to the UK until Baby G was eleven-weeks-old, at which point I was obliged to re-negotiate the parent's permission to observe their baby.

I first met Baby G himself when he was two days old, during weekly visits. I was struck by the difference in the baby after the father returned home, and by the problems experienced by his mother in accommodating a father for her child.

* * *

Mother tells me of her certainty from the beginning of her second pregnancy that she was carrying a daughter, and that this was the reason why she had wanted to have a lot of sexual intercourse with her partner at the time. During her third pregnancy however—Baby G—she sensed she was carrying a son, and states that this made her feel distant from his father. This may have accounted—at least in part—for father's absence from the sixth month of the pregnancy onwards, including the first eleven weeks of his son's life. I suspect that either mother felt she had a penis already inside her (and thus had no need for one from her partner) or else she felt anxious at the prospect of sexual intercourse because of the threat this would pose to her sense of bodily integration. However, as an observer, I was not in a position to discuss her fantasies with her.

Baby G's mother is very experienced and Baby G himself, who is breast-fed, is developing well. I notice that, at the age of nine weeks, Baby G looks tremendously pleased with himself. His mother, however, is scornful of his seemingly natural confidence, although I suspect that this scorn is actually aimed at maleness itself and that this might have been intensified by father's absence.

At ten weeks, a dullness appears in Baby G's eyes when his mother introduces a bottle and holds him away from her body during feeding. Both measures seem to me a preparation for father's homecoming. When Baby G urinates, his mother speedily collects the urine in her hand and throws it back into his face.

This, she explains, is a custom learnt from her mother, and that 'it is good for him'. She also reports that Baby G is hanging onto his faeces and seems frightened of urinating.

Mother's behaviour towards her child seemed to me an attack on the normal narcissism of her male infant. This may have arisen from a fear of the erect male organ and envy of it, given her upbringing in a family of women without men. I would not wish to suggest that *all* mothers attack their baby sons in this way. However, I think that all boys *are* subject to attacks of this kind, but that they usually take more subtle forms. In this case, it is not simply due to the fact that the mother comes from a female-dominated family. Instead her behaviour should be understood as something learnt to help her cope with *her own* deepest fears. Mother herself must feel in some way attacked (urinated on) by the baby's natural act, and so retaliated instantly. (Another custom mother describes to me concerns 'healing'; it involves putting breast-milk into the baby's eyes.)

At eleven weeks, then, father arrived home and mother rediscovered how lovely her baby was. Father brings order. For the first time since I began observing Baby G, the noisy television is turned off, which now seems to have had the function of filling the space left by father's absence. From this point Baby G become assertive and aggressive; he reaches out to his sister and to his toys, making new sounds. He uses his tongue, fingers, hands and teeth. As before, he plays at losing and rediscovering the breast, and touches and strokes it when he finds it.

There is intense competition between mother and father over who mothers Baby G. Mother is unhappy about stopping the breast-feeding, and Baby G is too. She blames the bottle for the baby's frequent vomiting. It seems to me that Baby G is sick from all that he is going through: feeling attached to his mother, meeting his father, losing the breast, and having to get used to bottle-feeding. At this point he begins to crawl.

At twelve weeks, when Baby G's crying reaches a high pitch, father goes over to him and lends the baby his fingers to play with, talking with him as he does so. Baby G's eyes are closed and he screams. He ignores his father's fingers but gradually notices his father's voice and calms down. When he stops crying father, who is now kneeling in front of him, gives Baby G his head to play with, so that father's head is now between baby's legs. Baby G pulls at his father's hair quietly for a moment or two, and then starts to cry again. Father picks him up impatiently, saying something like 'this is all you want' (meaning 'to be picked up'). Drying Baby G's tears, he places him on his shoulder. From this lofty position—which is, perhaps, where father himself would like to be—Baby G surveys the room.

By placing his head between the baby's legs, father may be acting out his own experience of being calmed. He may also be demonstrating his own need for sexual attention, projected into the baby. No sooner does father succeed in making Baby G comfortable than mother enters the room, saying that her breasts are tingling and this must have been caused by the baby's hunger. She takes Baby G away from father. Unconsciously, she seems to be making the point that she—not he—has the competence (that is, the breasts) where babies are concerned.

Mother sits on the floor and feeds Baby G, who uses both hands to hold the breast. Father becomes enraged as feeding begins and leaves the room. He dresses as if preparing to leave. Surprised by this, mother asks him if he is going out, which he confirms, busying himself. He comes over and kisses her and the children, says goodbye to me, and leaves the house boiling with anger. It seems that *someone* has to go, and that on this occasion it is father—although on a later occasion, at thirty-nine weeks, it will be Baby G himself who leaves. Baby G's mother seems to have no idea how to accommodate a father for her baby, whilst he himself is so frightened of his angry response to the emotional situation in which he finds himself that he has to remove himself, again and again...

At twenty weeks Baby G sits up and sleeps through the night. He allows his mother to leave the room without protesting, and plays with his feet, toes and fingers. Mother talks to me about how her baby needs the comfort of holding on to her. I noticed that, on being comforted, Baby G crosses his legs; he already seems to know he must protect his penis from attack.

At twenty-one weeks, mother offers her baby a dummy which later becomes a help to him. A few minutes into the observation he turns towards me and starts to cry. Mother takes him out of the recliner and lays him on his stomach on the floor. He holds onto her arm, and seems to be trying to keep hold of her. She stretches out on the floor near to him and, taking his dummy, she sucks it and holds it out to him. He takes it from her. She comments that Baby G really wants cuddles from her, and that he is now able to demand more from her because he can now physically hold on to her. It is as if, in her mind, he is rather larger than a baby. Baby G is working hard to keep her interested in him. He is also developing relationships with his father and siblings.

At twenty-two weeks, I observed the following: Father, by a quick movement with his right hand, and then with both hands, pulls Baby G towards him and sits him on father's stomach. Father pulls up his own legs and uses them as a back-rest for the baby. Father then withdraws his left hand and holds Baby G around the waist with his right hand. Baby G turns, reaching for father's left hand. It is not offered for him to play with. Baby G looks at his father enquiringly, holding back his head and scratching it. He makes another attempt to obtain his father's hand—the right one this time—but is unable to cause father to loosen his grip and offer his hand for play. Father jogs him up and down a few times. Baby G does not respond to this, but continues to look at father who now changes the baby's position. Father lays Baby G across father's stomach with Baby G's legs on the floor and his arms on father's chest. From this position Baby G looks over at me. Father constantly changes Baby G's position on or near to his own body. Baby G appears to be enjoying the physical closeness to his father, and does not seem to mind being moved about—except for one position, in which they lie side by side. Baby G's little hand holds his father's forearm, and father seems to be pinching it. When Baby G expresses his discomfort by making snuffling noises, father sits him up on the floor. At this point Baby G finds his own left foot, and begins playing with it.

I stand up, in order to see better. Father lifts Baby G back onto the cloth which is laid out for him on the floor, and rests him on his stomach. The pair have been together for half an hour, during which time father has not spoken to baby.

At thirty-nine weeks, mother informs me that father took Baby G to his uncle's house, in order to give him a break from his mother. Father feels that she and Baby G are too close, and that his mother is spoiling him. Baby G is left for a night and half a day with his uncle and aunt, who live at some distance. Mother is angry with father for doing this, but not sufficiently angry to prevent him. She accepts the situation, apparently with some awareness of the difficulties between herself, her husband and her child. In addition, to go and collect Baby G would imply that she distrusts her relatives.

Mother reports that, on his return, Baby G wanted to be cuddled—by his sister, most of all. It sounded to me likely that Baby G felt let down by both mother and father. Indeed, he continually turned to his sister and to me during the observation. Later, mother remarks that she thinks Baby G felt he had been dumped.

At forty-one weeks, Baby G suddenly became terrified. This occurred in the absence of his mother, but he seemed helped enormously by the presence of his three-year-old sister. It seems to me no coincidence that this experience occurred soon after his first separation from his mother and his father.

Baby G was standing at the rail at the back-door which leads to a landing two floors up, overlooking a large garden. He turns away into the bathroom and crawls over to the bath. He sits watching his sister and myself, but seems unintegrated. Something appears to be happening inside him, which may have come into his mind either whilst he was looking around outside, or on coming into the bathroom. In either case, it leaves him looking fragmented and unheld. He sits quite still, then stops looking at me and his sister and focuses instead on a point near to the ground—as if to steady himself—whilst making moaning noises. He leans forward, as if distressed, then puts his face into the carpet. He puts his left hand over his eyes, as if shutting me out or shutting out whatever is in his mind. He lies twisted up over one leg and cries into the carpet. Mother does not come, and he grows distraught. Looking back on this observation, I think now that he may very well have been remembering or re-experiencing the time he spent separated from his mother.

His sister is standing on a box at the hand-basin, playing at cleaning her teeth. She hears him and calls out his name, showing him the toothbrush she is holding. This pulls him out of the desperate state into which he has fallen. He looks up at her, seeming a little lost. Sensing the state he is in, she gets down from the box, goes over to him, and puts the toothbrush into his mouth. He smiles at her, then she walks back and climbs back up to the hand-basin. He continues to watch her and after a while crawls towards me. I am standing near the door. He comes and sits close by me, catching hold of his dummy and placing it expertly into his mouth, with his left hand. He regains his confidence through the use of the dummy, which has previously helped him establish a link to his mother.

Meanwhile, as Baby G's sister begins to come into her own as a little helper, something is happening to father.

At forty-three weeks father's anger over his powerlessness becomes evident in the way he begins to provoke Baby G. He does this—he tells me—with the express purpose of giving his baby 'a temper', because: 'he needs one to face life in this country'.

Father claims to see nothing wrong in deliberately provoking his baby into a tantrum, whilst mother expresses her concern that the baby will become 'too tough'. 'This country' to which father refers is not just the UK—it seems to me—but the deprived emotional environment which he feels he himself inhabits, alongside a partner who will not and cannot put him first.

Mother is not simply 'maternally preoccupied' in the Winnicottian sense,[12] she simply has no understanding of what it is that her partner needs in order to help him with his jealousy of the baby. Mother and father are locked together in feelings of intense frustration with one another.

Throughout my observation, mother seemed literally unable to attend to a partner as well as to her children—that is, to sexual as well as maternal demands. Her trouble seemed to lie in an over-identification with the infant. She herself appeared to have regressed to a kind of 'grown child'. At times it was quite difficult to differentiate between mother and children: she was often on the floor with the children, and there was a maximum of physical contact between her and them. This behaviour may have been partly connected with feeling abandoned by her partner at the end of the pregnancy and during the birth of Baby G. By excluding father she may have been trying to make him feel what she had felt during his absence. However, his response to experiencing her sense of loss was to turn to crude means of making her more adult. For instance, he asked her questions from an encyclopaedia in order to test her intelligence. Evidently he felt helpless in his attempts to regain his partner.

At forty-eight weeks, father's jealousy flared up again.

Baby G watches me from a standing position, holding onto a chair. His head is tilted to the right. Gradually he climbs up onto the seat of the chair and then onto his mother's legs. He kneels on mother's lap and she holds him lightly in her arms. Baby G makes a plunge forward, but mother draws him backwards so that he is now lying on top of her. Baby G proceeds to find his mother's mouth, then he opens his own mouth and kisses her. He takes his time over this, in a way which causes it to seem that he is making love with his mother. She responds in a similar manner, but then stops herself—protesting 'G, G!'—although it is evident she does not really want to stop. Baby G pauses for a moment, lays his head on her neck, and then turns towards me. Mother silently pulls at his hair as he lies there. Presently Baby G resumes his former activity, kissing mother a little more quickly. Mother starts to giggle.

The pair distract father from watching TV. He turns and throws a cushion at baby and mother, but she sees it coming and catches it. Baby G climbs down from his mother's lap and takes hold of the cushion. He looks at it, then at his father, and for a minute seems to be trying to work out what to do. Finally he places it on the floor next to his father, then he makes his way up the chair again and onto his mother's lap, and continues from where he left off.

Baby G is caught up in something that is both a delight and an agony—a situation perhaps not too dissimilar from Galton Flood's early relationship to his mother. Baby G's mother is strongly attached to her son, but seems to be using this in order to provoke father's jealousy. This also serves to prevent father from possessing her sexually, as well as keeping him away from his son. She seems to be making a statement that if there is going to be a triangular relationship between them, then *she* is not going to be the one left out. She herself, it should be remembered, had no experience of closeness with a father, and it is this which has left her unable to make room for the father that her own children need.

I would like to emphasise how this state of affairs—the exclusion of the father—occurs regardless of the physical presence of the father in the home. Men are often blamed for being absent and causing single-parenthood. However, to label 'irresponsible' a man who chooses to leave a situation such as this is to fail to understand the underlying psychodynamics.

Like Mr Flood, whose situation we considered in the previous chapter, the young father in this family suffers greatly. The provocation and the neglect he experiences threaten to swamp his adult self, to make him a baby too, and to cause him to function less well as an adult. By the end of Baby G's first year of life, it seems as if his mother is on the way to re-establishing herself as a single parent, like her mother and her grandmother before her.

Postscript

Father became increasingly depressed and left the family when Baby G was four-years-old. After leaving, he did not support the children in the way that the first baby's father had done— because, I think, he was too angry with mother to be able to do so.

Baby G was robbed of an important life-experience, of growing up with a loving and well-functioning parental couple. As a result, the resolution of Baby G's Oedipus complex is likely to face complications. Having won an empty victory over his father, Baby G, as the preferred male, will always fear retaliative attack from father in the future. In addition, there will always be anxiety over his mother's power to castrate him—which, in this case, dates back to the tenth week of his life. Any of these factors could leave G susceptible to psychological disturbance when he reaches mid-adolescence.

As we have seen previously, the type of family patterns discussed in this chapter are partly due to the trauma of enslavement endured by Africans in the Caribbean, and partly due to the ways in which individuals have dealt with the legacy of that trauma. Removed from the Caribbean to the UK, or to the US, or elsewhere, the child without a father, and without a family network in which someone might take on the function of father, loses the means to become separate from mother. This is the context which threatens rebellious boys, in particular, with the prospect of early criminalisation. There is often no helpful, holding influence *between* the closeness to mother at home (from which they attempt to break out, in order to individuate) and the heavy hand of the Law and the State. Baby G's father appreciated this problem well enough, very early on, as is evidenced in his attempt to banish baby from mother. However, he—like his wife's partner before him—could do nothing constructive to alter the situation.

Non-rebellious boys, on the other hand, often continue to live with their mother, long after they literally need to do so. For a man to live with his mother after he has had children protects him in several ways: from having to cope with intense feelings of jealousy; from having to be assertive and aggressive towards women; and from having to cope with being separate and living alone.

I have no doubt that there are always economic and social factors which contribute to these situations but, as I see it, the psychological reasons—the *choices* people make—are by far the more powerful, and it is these which form my main concern.

Chapter Six

A Little Girl's Story[13]

Although people of Caribbean origin—and other African people—have lived in the UK for centuries, there is a shared belief among the British (of all colours) that blacks are newly arrived.[14]

The Caribbean people who arrived in the UK in the 1950s and in the early 1960s—that is, during the height of post-Second World War migration—entered a world of full employment. They left behind countries which had recently become independent, or were in the process of becoming so. Like most immigrants, they came in search of a better life—economically speaking. They had a set of priorities and values different from those of the English working class, alongside whom most of them lived. Even to this day, the professionals with whom people of Caribbean origin come into contact—that is, teachers, social workers, careers officers—sometimes regard the desires and aspirations of these children and their parents as crazy and unrealistic. To such professionals, people of Caribbean origin sometimes appear not to know 'their place'. For instance, Caribbean parents were complaining bitterly and vociferously about the education their children were receiving some thirty years before their indigenous neighbours protested and action was finally taken to improve standards. A defeatist attitude prevailed amongst the indigenous working class: that poverty-stricken neighbourhoods should be *expected* to contain hopeless schools, and that this is one's lot in life.

This period of migration to the UK occurred alongside British de-colonisation and political re-alignment, in the course of which there was a swapping of 'alienships'. The people who were formerly 'aliens'—that is, who lived in countries across the English Channel—were suddenly on their way to becoming fellow citizens of the European Economic Community. Meanwhile, people who were formerly subjects of the British Empire in many cases lost their rights of citizenship in a profound sense, and have been fighting for them ever since. It is always possible to become 'alien' in a political sense, even if one was born within the EEC. Politicians of the far-right have not failed to notice this discrepancy, and to build power bases upon it.

Naturally, these changes have had important consequences on the personal as well as the social. For instance, a new language of ethnicity and race has developed; new words have appeared with new meanings. 'Ethnic' is used to mean 'black' or 'brown'. Alongside the term 'ethnic minority' has appeared a school of thought which assumes that all the people belonging to this group should be lumped together and provided for outside the mainstream—that is, outside the realm of 'the majority'. However, even at the risk of racial stereotyping, it has to be said that groups which are currently monied do not seem to feature within the 'ethnic minority' frame. An entire industry has been established which claims to serve the needs of so-called 'ethnic minorities', although I am not suggesting that the people who work within it necessary adhere to the type of world-view I have described. The first challenges to this world-view seem to me likely to arise from those who feel unable to fit into the prevailing official categories of personhood—that is, children and adults of *mixed* ethnicity who (for example) may *look* like people of Caribbean origin, but in fact have no links or ties to the region.

Migration also revived a conception which dates back to slavery —namely, that 'family' is not confined to immediate blood relatives; that 'family' is any group of people which comes together in order to make do. For instance, I came to know of a female lodger who provided the household support system for a wife and husband who were caring for a difficult foster child. The child was, in fact, the daughter of the husband's deceased best friend. The two men were from the same country and had shared a room when they first arrived in the UK. The child—a girl—with her father dead, and her mother mentally ill, had to be cared for by people other than her parents, if she was not to end up with strangers in the care of the local authority.

Unfortunately, stories of how *well* people *can* manage, even in extremely difficult circumstances, rarely become widely known. When familial dysfunction occurs—however—it is often a disaster for the child. What follows is a discussion of a case of this type.

* * *

Miss C was born into an extended family network. In general, families of Caribbean origin enjoy a greater variety of structures than indigenous European families, but basically there are three types: the two-parent nuclear type, with one or more generations; the extended network, in which both women and men involve themselves in caring for the children; and the extended network which is headed by women, and in which women take sole charge of caring for the children—sometimes including the children of several generations.

Viewing an individual against the background of their 'family type' sometimes helps in understanding the problems they present. I have found that, as a general rule, where there is a problem with a family of the 'extended network' type, then the children seem to suffer particularly badly.

Miss C, who was in her late twenties, came with a problem which involved her anger sometimes getting out of control. Her mother was the chief object of her anger. Miss C had never had a boyfriend, and feared men. She became concerned about herself when a friend's mother remarked to her and the friend—as they were leaving to go out to a club—'see that you girls don't frighten the men away'. She was also experiencing trouble sleeping, and suffered from bouts of asthma and eczema.

In terms of her family history, Miss C was the eldest child born in the UK to parents who had migrated from the Caribbean. Her parents had left all their previous children behind with relatives. Father arrived first in the UK, and later mother joined him. The couple connected up with relatives on the husband's side—who were already settled in the UK—and moved into a room in a house owned by an uncle. Other rooms in the house were occupied by other members of the extended family. Miss C was born into this tightly packed house, in which her immediate family lived in a single room, whilst the rest of the house was filled with her extended family.

The emotional environment of her early life was haunted by lost children, and the missing figures of other significant family members—particularly her grandparents, on both sides. I suspect that Miss C's mother may have been undergoing an experience not dissimilar to that of a mother whose other children had died; she had neither her children nor her own mother by her side.

As a small child, Miss C was minded by 'a woman living down the road' whilst both her parents went to work. During the school holidays she was left in the house with whomever happened to be at home—as she put it, '*someone* in the house looked after me'. There was never one *particular* person who had responsibility for her in her parent's absence. My belief is that she felt completely abandoned by her parents during these times. Even as a child she suffered from eczema, which she associated with states of stress. Her asthma, however, she believed was due to an allergy.

During Miss C's early adolescence, her father was diagnosed as schizophrenic—although she could not remember exactly when. Her father must have been unwell some time before the diagnosis, and was probably too afraid to move away from his extended family—which must have taken the place of his mother in his mind. Miss C's mother may have colluded in the isolation of Miss C's father; nevertheless, father underwent repeated hospital admissions, which necessitated increasingly more lengthy stays in hospital.

Miss C's father was the youngest child in his family, and grew up with his widowed mother. His father died in a boating accident when he was three-years-old. Miss C's widowed grandmother was said to have been an Obeah woman—a woman in touch with the supernatural—and to have tied her son to her by means of magical powers. She had disapproved of his marriage to Miss C's mother.

Prior to his marriage, Miss C's father made repeated attempts to leave his mother, by travelling to work in other countries in the Caribbean, and in the USA, although he always returned to his mother, with money which she added to a bank account that she kept for him. His mother died just after his first admission to the psychiatric hospital in the UK. Miss C informed me that her grandmother had used up all the money in her father's bank account before her death. When news of this reached her father, his condition took a turn for the worse. His delusions concerned Mrs. Thatcher and the Queen stealing his property, whilst his mother—it seemed—remained beyond reproach. I believe that when his mother died, Miss C's father perhaps lost all hope of having his infantile needs met; he must have felt robbed of absolutely everything. It is possible that—with the early death of his father—he was misused by his mother when he was a small child, as a means of comforting her in her distress, perhaps extending to actual, physical sexual abuse.

Miss C's mother, meanwhile, was the eldest child of parents who never married; her father was already promised to another woman at the time he met her mother, and so he did not stay with her. Miss C's mother therefore grew up without a father, and was looked after by her mother and grandmother. Probably she had absolutely no childhood experience of closeness to a male family-member. Consequently, then, both Miss C's parents grew up in families in which there were no fathers, and no available ongoing experience of a heterosexual couple.

Miss C's family lived in overcrowded conditions, with the extended family in the uncle's house, until they were re-housed by the local council—firstly in a flat, and then a house. The latter had important psychological implications for the father; he broke down soon after they moved.

During the time Miss C lived with her extended family, she was sexually abused on at least three occasions. On the first, she was left alone with her uncle—also her godfather—who sexually assaulted her by having full intercourse with her. She was threatened with further assaults if she told her mother. On the second occasion, she could remember being left with a female family-member who lived nearby. This woman went out, leaving her alone in the house with a male family-member, who was visiting. He took the opportunity of the woman's absence to assault the little girl. On another occasion she was molested by the same man and a visiting friend of the family.

In addition, she told me of a particularly frightening experience she had endured in a lift on the way up to her parents' flat. She also told me how, during her childhood, she had witnessed the sexual assault of a female cousin—the same age as herself—by one of the men who had previously abused her.

In telling her story, she did not present her father as someone to whom she could turn, and she did not attempt to tell her mother about the abuse. She did once mention to her mother that she was 'hurting in the middle'; her mother did not enquire any further what this meant, but took her to the family doctor. Reportedly, the doctor asked if she was drinking enough and, when he was told that she drank a lot of fruit squash, he advised her mother to give her more water to drink instead. She was never examined by either the GP or her mother.

Miss C did well at school and went to university, where she completed a degree. Like many other students at that time, she did not immediately obtain employment. Her eczema returned whilst she was out of work. Fearing unemployment less than being alone and dying of emotional starvation, she returned home, and felt unable to leave afterwards. However, she then quickly obtained a job, and was still doing the same work when she came to see me some years later. She was also experiencing difficulties with moving on from this job, even though it was in her professional best interests to do so.

* * *

Before turning to details of the events which led her to seek help, I shall discuss some ideas relating to the theme of consultation in psychotherapy, and will mention a few points which I have found very useful in establishing a map of the patient's inner world.

With patients of Caribbean origin, I have found it is sometimes helpful to encourage the patient to speak about experiences of 'good health' and 'bad health' as a means of gaining access to the patient's inner world. I have found that patients from this background are often particularly well-tuned into their bodies, and are often willing to speak about their bodies in detail. For instance, in my consultation with Miss C I found it useful to focus on Miss C's physical actions—her 'action language' as it were—as well as on her feelings, since her thoughts in the session were often muddled, forgotten, or impossible to put into words. This helped circumvent the problem whether Miss C was a 'suitable patient' for psychotherapy—that is, psychotherapy conceived as a treatment which is focused mainly upon 'talking'—in an environment in which psychotherapeutic treatment was in short supply. In my opinion patients like Miss C, who have experienced difficulties in the parenting they received, or who have endured traumatic experiences, are quite unable to express their dis-ease in mentalistic terms.

What should also be borne in mind is the evidence that patients of Caribbean origin often come to the attention of mental health services only when they are in the most acute stages of mental illness, at which point they are usually ill enough to be admitted to hospital. For example, A.W. Burke (1984) conducted a study of West Indians in Aston, Birmingham, and observed that cases of depression amongst this group went undiagnosed by GPs. He also observed—based on five years of data obtained from GPs—that there was a higher percentage of psychosomatic disorders among West Indians. Burke concluded that:

> ... even when GPs are fully experienced in the management of everyday problems of life and illness, they have an uncanny tendency to underdiagnose psychological problems when confronted with West Indian patients. (Burke 1984: 57-8)

It would seem, then, that some patients from certain cultural backgrounds have their own particular ways of describing what they think is happening to themselves; that there is little distinction between what is psychological and what is somatic; and that, in these circumstances, patients are not in a position to help their GPs diagnose the problem. However, it should not be concluded that *all* patients with a Caribbean origin have this 'problem'. They do not. Instead, this would seem to depend on the type of family structure, and on the type of emotional experience they had—as an infant—within this structure.

In this context, I have found the ideas of Joyce McDougall very useful (McDougall 1989). She writes on the importance of the father in helping the infant cope with the fact of difference, and indicates how the presence of the father helps the infant (1) separate what is somatic from what is psychological, and (2) cope with the task of separating its own body, sex and mind from its mother's body, sex and mind (McDougall 1989: 32-49). McDougall regards this experience as originating from the internalised, good-enough father *in the mind of the mother*, as she cares for her child, as well as from the actual presence of the good-enough father and the presence of the good-enough couple. It is the psychical structures engendered by these types of experience which patients of Caribbean origin, who have had no early experience of good-enough fathering, might be said to lack. In some cases, this lack may span several generations.

* * *

Three years before coming to see me, Miss C began to experience problems on a physical level. Her sinuses became blocked, and she suffered from a constantly runny nose. Mucus would pour through her eyes when she blew her nose. She went to see her doctor, and he referred her to an ENT specialist. This consultation was followed by surgery, during which the lining of her nostrils was removed. However, the blockage and the runny nose continued.

It was after the failure of surgery to cure this problem that she first had what she came to call 'the faces dream'. She was unsure whether she was asleep or awake, but at the end of the experience she screamed, which brought her mother hurrying into her bedroom. The dream was of *three clouds floating across her room, each with a face in its midst*. She was terrified.

This dream—which may well have been a hallucination—was a matter of great concern to the rest of Miss C's family. Members of the extended family discussed it together, and a plan was drawn up to attend to the spirits which family members believed were bothering Miss C, rather than to attend to Miss C herself. It was suggested that she should change the position of her bed, because at that time it was facing the door, thus encouraging the spirits to interfere with her. I found it interesting that although the idea of someone 'interfering' with Miss C was present, it was projected onto the idea of 'bad spirits'.

In co-operating with the family's remedy for her problem, it seemed to me that Miss C was attempting to find a way of preventing the trauma she had experienced from forcing itself into her consciousness and destroying her mind. The family required her to hide herself from the spirits, by positioning her bed so that its head blocked the entrance to her room, and so that she was facing the wall. This—it was said—would baffle the spirits, and thus prevent their entry into her body as well as her mind. The sexual symbolism of this manoeuvre is, I think, obvious.

Miss C attempted to sleep in this fashion for three years, but at the end of that time had developed a painful shoulder along the side on which she rested. She felt that she could lay in this position no longer. An additional difficulty arose from the fact that she had been anally abused, so turning over and laying on her other side still (it seemed to her) left her vulnerable to attack. It was part of her attempt to gain relief from this situation which contributed to her coming to see me.

Two years before the first consultation, Miss C's mother and father had separated, although this was not openly acknowledged within the family. Her father had gone into permanent community care. Then, a year before the consultation, Miss C and her mother had jointly bought the council house, to which the family had been transferred during her early adolescence. The purchase had been Miss C's idea, and her mother had been very pleased with her daughter. However, over that year her anger towards her mother had begun to mount steadily, as a consequence of the responsibility she had taken on. Miss C felt that her mother was unappreciative of her efforts to please, and she spoke of the way her mother imposed upon her, both financially and emotionally.

Underlying these financial arrangements was a wish to find 'security'. I think that both Miss C and her mother were extremely anxious over the prospect of separation. Miss C has passed through a troubled childhood, and had arrived at adolescence totally unprepared for the challenges which faced her. The terror she had experienced at becoming an independent person had sent her back to her family, and had kept her there. With her father unwell her mother had come to rely upon her for both financial and emotional support. Miss C, having missed out on age-appropriate attention from her mother and father, had formed a couple with her mother. The purchase of the house sealed their union. From this position Miss C could begin to attack her mother 'on a stable basis', safe in the knowledge that she could not be thrown out of a house which was—in effect—her own. She literally paid the price—that is, the mortgage—for being able to continue her sadistic attacks, although these—if left untreated—might in time drive her mad too.

The reason for the establishment of this abusive couple seemed to be Miss C's anger over her emotional neglect and abuse at the hands of her parents. Miss C was using her salary not to nurture herself and her mother, not to pay for her house and her therapy, but primarily to establish on a firmer basis this sadomasochistic couple within which she could continue to be a child, and could continue to attack the internal parents who had failed her. Outwardly, however, she appeared the perfect, supportive, good daughter, to be envied by the parents of bad daughters everywhere. Miss C's mother, meanwhile, was paying the price for refusing to help her daughter separate from her, which included living at close quarters with a trapped, resentful daughter, who might one day murder her. A household such as this could only fall into ruin, over the course of time.

This rage at the mother, at her failure to protect the daughter as a child, is indeed murderous. It is the kind of rage which descends back through the generations to the beginnings of the modern Caribbean, and then beyond the seas back to Africa. Deep down, Caribbean Africans feel angry towards Africans for failing to protect them from abuse, and for co-operating with Europeans in their enslavement.

Miss C's rage was also the kind of rage that either drives people to become mad or to become bad. The level of her disturbance required psychoanalytic psychotherapy rather than counselling, which is what—initially—she had requested. Her sadistic attacks on her mother put her in danger of destroying all her good objects, and of joining her father in the mental hospital. Even so, the function of her rage must also have been to maintain a *kind* of sanity. How else could sanity have been maintained in previous generations during times of slavery?

It seemed that Miss C's sexual impulses and fantasies, which were normally kept under tight control, came to the surface after the remark made by her friend's mother. Gradually, this threatened to overwhelm her. It was this burst of awakened feeling which threatened to push her into psychosis, and which was accompanied by more open, angry attacks on her mother, and the dream of the faces—which might have been an hallucination or a post-traumatic nightmare.

Herbert Rosenfeld, drawing on his work with psychotic patients, makes some important observations which are relevant in connection with Miss C. He suggests that during the acute schizophrenic state, the splitting of the ego actually *lessens*. The acute schizophrenic state, he argues, leads to states of intense confusion, but also to attempts to reconstruct the ego and object relations in a more beneficial way (Rosenfeld 1963: 159). He also notes that sexual impulses and fantasies in the acute psychotic state become unbearable, because they are accompanied by overwhelmingly strong murderous and sadistic fantasies (Rosenfeld 1963: 165). It is my belief that—if left untreated—this young woman might well have had to choose between becoming completely paranoid (like Galton Flood) or, alternatively, of placing herself in what I prefer to call 'a state of avoidance', in which sexuality is denied and there is no possibility of heterosexual coupling.

Miss C knew from experience that none of the family's attempted 'solutions' would work for her—which had driven her to seek help outside the family. Here was a woman who danced alone, but who could not understand why this should be so when there were men willing to dance with her. She was dissatisfied with the situation in which she found herself but could see no way out—which made her intensely miserable.

On her father's side of her family, emotional problems like these were dealt with by means of rituals and attempts to control bad spirits, located outside the self. This 'doing' avoided the necessity of 'thinking', and represents a distortion of African tradition in the post-slavery Caribbean. On her mother's side of the family, appeals were made to the Church in times of stress. After a bad dream Miss C's mother, a Roman Catholic, would tell her to pray and to make sure she went to church on Sunday. This might be taken to represent the 'European' tradition in the Caribbean. In effect, then, the legacy of both parents was the idea that salvation comes from somewhere *outside* the self.

When patients bring to their sessions stories which, on the surface, appear to demonstrate no concept of an internal world, or which make them appear incapable of understanding symbolism, then they do not appear suitable for psychoanalytic psychotherapy. Instead they bring what appears to be (according to Joyce McDougall) a *body* that is going mad—in other words, psychosomatosis. I do not wish to claim here that all psychosomatosis is treatable. However, by failing to take these patients into treatment we may be failing to take up the opportunity to discover more about how the mind develops, and failing to provide relief to a group of people in terrible distress.

Miss C, who had clearly been in serious difficulties for some years, was never referred for psychotherapeutic help of any kind. She regularly presented herself to her doctor, with bodily symptoms, and was treated as a physical case. Once she heard about a place in which she *could* receive something different, she made a self-referral.

Referral difficulties cannot be placed solely at the door of the helping agencies and individual therapists. My first contact with Miss C's mother—when I returned Miss C's first call—made me feel as if I had committed a terrible intrusion. The initial questioning this provoked in me—as to why I was seeing Miss C alone, and not with her mother—I later understood as a clue to the difficulties which Miss C presented. She enjoyed absolutely no privacy and respect as a separate person who might want to take her own telephone messages. Miss C herself seemed likely to try to use her family to sabotage the treatment, and the members of her family themselves were unlikely to support her therapy.

Thought itself was extremely painful for Miss C. She used forgetting and confusion in order to avoid pain. She communicated an intense passivity, implying that now she had told me her story it was up to me to make her feel better. The idea of working together as equal participants in a couple was completely foreign to her. She was not able to pay the usual fee, which was—in part—a reflection of the state of her internal resources. Indeed, it seemed unlikely she would be able to find any resources inside herself until she could disengage from the internal, sadomasochistic relationship with her mother. In terms of the transference, it was hell at times, due to the way in which the attacking part of her was only the topmost layer of an enormous depression.

I will list here some of the obstacles to treatment presented by patients of Caribbean origin, although it can be seen that some of these are not at all peculiar to this ethnic group:

1. Suspicion within the Caribbean community of the other—that is, of white people—and very little experience of taking problems outside the family.

2. An over-dependent relationship with the mother (who is not in therapy).

3. Borderline symptoms, which include psychosomatising, confusional states, and hallucinations.

4. High levels of projection of parts of the self (for example, in the form of 'spirits'). These may be regarded as a contra-indication to psychotherapy. However, is this a defence employed to keep 'craziness' outside, or could it be that—alongside high levels of projection—there has developed the capacity to succeed in holding the good parts of the self alongside the bad parts?

5. Lack of support, sympathy, and knowledge in the family about psychotherapy, coupled with an authoritarian, rather than a democratic, family structure.

6. The fact that the patient is often the family breadwinner, and so financial and emotional resources are sometimes limited.

7. Difficulties for the therapist of entering into a cultural background which is unknown, different, or—possibly—closed.

8. Lack of interest on the part of the therapist in working with patients who do not currently fall within the 'ideal patient' category.

9. Difficult technical problems for the therapist—for example, being called upon to work with people who have been physically sexually abused; and being forced to realise that people can think differently from oneself yet still be adjudged 'sane', that personal experiences of high levels of control by external forces may be regarded as a norm by some people.

Taken on balance these considerations—which *all* apply in the case of Miss C—may have prevented a referral. However, they are not the whole story. On the plus side, this woman had survived some terrible experiences; she possessed some insight and had developed the capacity to take care of herself and others, no matter how muddled and split she became. This capacity shone through. She was intelligent, was capable of making links, and capable of allowing me to make links for her. She could translate the concrete into the meaningful; for instance, it was she who made the connection between the literally emptied bank account and her father's state of mind, which indicated a degree of psychological understanding. In addition, she was interested in talking about her vivid 'dream of the faces'; she had friends and was capable of making more; she was not in the grip of an intellectual defence; and she knew that she was ill, and recognised that it was her feelings of intense pain which made her inflict pain on others. Taken together, then, these constitute a list of good indicators for psychotherapy.

In the world of Miss C's childhood the normal boundary between child and adult was shattered. Both parents and children were physically crammed together in a single room, without sufficient psychical separation. In addition, the extended family presented an actual danger to the child. Miss C's parents were unable to protect her from sexual abuse and to keep her safe, whilst maintaining their place within the extended family. If her father had insisted on protecting his child, this might have resulted in his eviction from the extended family in both a physical and a psychical sense. The situation seems similar to that between Miss C's father and his mother. Indeed, it might have been his hatred towards his mother which prevented him from developing protective feelings towards his daughter. It is my belief that this hatred literally drove him mad. Miss C's mother was similarly unable to protect her daughter from sexual abuse, and apparently powerless to reclaim the older children whom she had left behind in the Caribbean. It seems possible, however, that she was in fact protecting the other children from abuse by refusing to reunite the family.

The conditions in which child sexual abuse can thrive were evident everywhere in the emotional and physical environment in which this patient grew up. I suspect that some of the confusions which surround the diagnosis of schizophrenia in patients of Caribbean origin are in fact rooted in the consequences of sexual abuse, which seems to create borderline states of mind. Perhaps it is the case that the feelings engendered by traumatic displacements cause human beings—whatever their race or culture—to behave in an unusual way towards their young.

I would not be surprised if Miss C's father was in fact aware that his daughter was being sexually abused, or if he himself had also abused her. Perhaps he was abused as a child; like girls, boys can be abused by their mothers, or by other female relatives, in the absence of husbands. It is no coincidence that child-

Chapter Seven

Masculinity in Crisis

The neuroses of women of Caribbean origin cannot be considered in isolation from the troubles of the men. However, it seems to me that the difficulties which men and women experience in relating to one another are external as well as internal.

For instance, externally there are the difficulties presented by the effects of slavery, migration, racial prejudice, and discrimination. These lead to disruption of the established systems for social intercourse, and entail that alternative systems have to be built instead. For young adults there are the additional external difficulties of leaving home and living independently, which are exacerbated by unemployment and the lack of an adequate income. Freud himself was quite clear on the importance of work (Freud 1930: 101), yet independent research has revealed the heavy burden of unemployment which young black people—especially men—have to bear. Figures for the UK in May 1996 indicate that 36 per cent of black men aged 16-24-years were unemployed, compared with 17 per cent of white men (Institute of Race Relations 1999).

As I hope to illustrate in this chapter, patterns of relationship travel down through the generations. A child, whose migrant family is confronted with the new environment of the UK, in which the external world makes many more demands upon the individual, is not helped if his family places prohibitions on his early attempts to explore his unfamiliar surroundings. However, parents in this situation do become anxious about the safety of their children—especially the safety and survival of their sons, and with good reason. As the case of Stephen Lawrence demonstrates, young black men are sometimes murdered, and sometimes their murderers go free. The social setting, therefore, can have a devastating impact on the personal. Yet the protective response of parents to external situations can create distortions in the relationship between mothers and their sons, and thus between women and men. In some cases, the bond between the parents and the children becomes stronger than that between the married couple. As a consequence, children often feel trapped by their parents or a particular parent, and experience extreme difficulty in separating from them physically and psychically. Often the child is unable to locate precisely where the prohibition comes from—that is, whether it originates from inside the self, or whether it actually comes from the parents. The inability to move away and into families of their own is quite widespread among patients of Caribbean origin and, to my mind, is quite definitely connected with the prevalence of mental ill health among this group.

* * *

D, in his late thirties, came from a family which lacked solid support from the extended family. He spent his early years in a Caribbean country where his mother—with the help of a maternal aunt—cared for him. He did not know his natural father. He had a brother, three years older, who had been left in charge of him as far back as he could remember.

When D was six years old, both his mother and his aunt were married and—with their husbands and the two boys—came to live in the UK. On their arrival the two sisters set up homes separately, and embarked upon new and different lives. D's family had trouble finding affordable housing, and moved around for some time until they settled. The distance from home to workplace was much greater for everyone in the household than in the old country. The regulations of industrialised work, and the climate, also had to be accommodated. Because she left home early in the morning and returned home late, D saw much less of his mother than before. In the winter months the loss of sunlight at both ends of the day played havoc with everyone's mood. D retained some memories of his stepfather collecting him from school, but usually he was the last child to leave the playground at the end of the day.

Around this time, D's stepfather began staying out late and drinking, and there was a lot of quarrelling between his parents. The stepfather left home on a few occasions, and finally left for good when D was twelve-years-old. This upset him very much, and he felt robbed of what little support he had. He experienced his mother as both physically and emotionally unavailable. There was a strict code within the household of keeping family business completely private. On the occasion he was overheard telling a school-friend that his stepfather had left, D's brother beat him up.

D's relationship with his stepfather seems to have been very ambivalent. On several occasions he stole food which his mother had prepared and left for his stepfather—and then denied having done so. He stated that he liked his stepfather, and believed he was a caring person. At an unconscious level, perhaps, he was trying to acquire potency by stealing from *both* his mother and stepfather. D had the impression that his mother hated his stepfather. His evidence for this was that she would say 'God bless him' when it seemed to D she actually meant 'God curse him'. He reported that his mother was generally contemptuous of his stepfather and of other men; however, D himself feared her and avoided all confrontations with her.

After her husband left, D's mother became an enthusiastic churchgoer, and formed a special relationship with the pastor. Much to D's resentment, money—which could have been spent on treats for her sons—was donated to the church. His mother had no further partners.

The themes I mentioned earlier—concerning the parent's lack of respect for the separateness of the child—are particularly evident in the case of D. For instance, throughout his childhood D and his brother shared a bed. The sole reason for this was his mother's wish for her children to be 'close' to one another; she took special pleasure in seeing her boys hugging one another whilst they slept. Indeed, D would sometimes do this just to please her, if he heard her approaching their room. This fully grown child sometimes slept with his parents in their bed, and—at least once—pretended to be asleep whilst his mother and stepfather made love. After his stepfather left he continued to sleep with his mother, until well into adolescence. There was no one to put a stop to this. As in the case of Baby G., father 'lost the war'.

When D's aunt experienced marital problems of her own, and her husband left, D was asked by his mother to look after her. She had no children, and so he shared her bed with her. Even though he was an adolescent at the time, he readily agreed to do what his mother asked. The reasoning behind the arrangement was that the aunt could not possibly be left alone, and had to have someone to sleep with her. I think this serves as a graphic illustration of how seriously anxiety about separation was treated and experienced in this family: two adult women agreed to share between them this young, adolescent boy.

At school D began to under-achieve. His work grew progressively worse as he became older. Even though the school he attended was itself under-performing—like many in the neighbourhood—I suspect that a contributory factor to his educational difficulties was the way in which schoolwork must have seemed dull in comparison to the serious 'work' of the adult world (that is, caring for his mother and aunt) in which he was involved at home.[16]

As the emotional burden on D increased, so did his physical weight, and he began to hate his body. This provided him with a reason to retreat more and more from socialising with his peers and his bother. He spent almost the entirety of his young adult life in isolation from his peer group, staying at home to help his mother in the house, or else retreating into his own world of fantasies. At this stage—he stated—he thought he liked girls, but 'did not know what to do with them', which seemed to indicate the opposite. He also had problems with a desire to expose himself in public—and in fact did so on several occasions. This wish was strongest in him after spending nights with his aunt.

D's mother considered him a 'good son', unlike his brother, who was always out with his friends and at risk of running into trouble with the police. Actually, his brother never was in any trouble, but his mother's anxiety persisted nonetheless. Like many Caribbean mothers—alone, with no husband to share worries about the children—D's mother worried about her son becoming a criminal and being imprisoned. Indeed, the boys were in trouble, but in a purely psychical sense. D's manner of relating to his family developed along the lines of saying and doing the complete opposite to what he actually felt. Naturally, he brought this way of relating along to his psychotherapy sessions. He believed it was a means of gaining and maintaining a special place in his mother's attention. He was extremely identified with her yet—at the same time—hated her. This hatred served the function of keeping them apart, and subduing his feelings of excitement towards her.

D's normal capacity for aggression was held in check by his dependence upon his mother, and his knowledge that she could not be swayed or bullied. When he did succeed—rather late in life—to move out of his mother's house and into the outside world, with the support of a female friend, he was unable to take anything good with him into his new home. He continued to feel isolated and troubled by disturbing fantasies. His relationships were entirely superficial, and often conducted mostly over the telephone. Although he started to feel that he was homosexual, he could not bring himself to form a relationship with an adult male. He worried that he might abuse children. It was a fear of dying, and of not being discovered until some time after his death, which brought him to seek therapy.

* * *

The absence of his father, the desertion of both his stepfather and his uncle, had left D at risk of abuse from his own mother and his aunt. His mother's refusal to acknowledge that D and his brother were young men filled him with extreme rage. He was kept by his mother in a permanent state of frustration, yet also in a state of dependency. On the one hand his passion was inflamed, and on the other he was kept deprived of satisfaction. This deeply humiliating experience left him with a strong desire to control other people. Men sometimes seek a heterosexual exit from this kind of situation by making a bee-line towards a relationship with a woman who is somehow 'other'—preferably a passive, white woman. However, woe betide this woman if she fails to live up to his conscious or unconscious expectations of her!

The difficulties experienced by parents in forming a couple, together with the breakdown of extended family networks, place enormous loads on boys and young men, who are then at risk of being used to replace adult men. Of course, this situation does not arise in *all* families without a father. What seems most decisive is the quality of the mother's relationship with her own father in her own mind. There may be a link between outbreaks of 'madness' or 'badness' in boys without fathers during their adolescence, but in at least some cases these are desperate attempts to resolve unbearable internal conflict, and may serve the useful purpose of removing the young man physically from his home. Although it is not my aim to minimise the good job that most single parenting mothers perform, or to ignore the criminalisation of deprived, young, black males by society in general, it seems to me difficult to overestimate the chances of a man with D's experiences growing up psychologically healthy. This man reached physical maturity with very little sense of what it is to be a person with his own mind, body, and sexuality. His identification with his mother was an attempt to avoid the pain of separation—which, however, might have been bearable, were it not for the intense hatred he felt towards her.

Fathers—or other individuals who might perform the father function (perhaps an aunt, uncle, or strict grandmother)—are essential to successive generations, who require them for the specific purpose of helping the infant towards an experience of difference. Without this, difficulties concerning psychological separateness are likely to arise. Individuals in a situation similar to that of D are likely to experience trouble distinguishing between their own body, sex, and mind, and that of their mother. The achievement of separate identity enables the individual to find a way of being alone without feeling dreadful loneliness. Separation opens up the possibility of non-parasitic, more healthy ways of relating.

Chapter Eight

Parental Distress and Childhood Disturbance

At thirteen-months-old, Little S, and his family, were referred to child guidance by a doctor at a mother and baby clinic. Both parents had visited the clinic at the father's insistence. He was concerned about Little S's behaviour: he was throwing food around, rocking, and head-banging against the side of his cot. The referring doctor mentioned that—physically—Little S was developing satisfactorily, and seemed well-cared for.

The family—father, mother, S the older son, and Little S— arrived for their first appointment half-an-hour late. Father was very reluctant to come in and see me, and only came in when Older S asked him to do so. I was struck by how extremely unhappy both the parents looked. Mother was thirty-five years old. She looked young for her age, and wore her hair in a girlish style. Father, however, looked all of his forty-one years.

Father began by telling me that he thought his son had a medical problem and should see a doctor. At this, mother gave father a look of contempt and pointed out that S had already been to the doctor. However, they were both worried about their child and agreed that his behaviour was growing worse. They described how S was rocking and banging his head first on one end, and then at the other end of his cot. He was also covering his ears, as if he had earache. When he rocked the noise he made travelled throughout their house.

Mother thought and hoped that he would grow out of the symptoms, which began when Little S was five-months-old. Father explained that the symptoms were a replacement for cry-ing, and expressed an idea that their son simply needed com-fort. He sought to provide this for Little S by offering him a dummy, and a touch of brandy at night. Mother disagreed with these arrangements, and the couple had proceeded to impose their conflicting solutions upon their baby.

Mother was against allowing children to become dependent on sucking for comfort. She believed that, once it was estab-lished, such a dependency could not be broken. Father thought the habit could be controlled, as long as Little S was not allowed to have the dummy for more than six months. Each was convinced they were right, and each was intent on putting the other in the wrong. This lead to noisy quarrelling, which flooded the clinic in much the same way as the sound of the baby's head-banging filled their home. This arguing over comfort seemed to me a defence against depression; they could not agree on whether they even ought to allow comfort to be given.

Father seemed to possess some real warmth for his little son, and had an intellectual understanding of certain theories of relationships. He was, however, as contemptuous of his partner, as she was of him. I asked why they were still together. 'Things could not be worse', replied father, laughingly, but not without some evident despair.

To me it seemed that Little S was attempting to contain his parents' distress by rocking. I put it to them that Little S was showing his distress at their distress, but father replied that he was too young to know about this. Mother grew angrier, expressing her growing dissatisfaction with father. She felt undervalued, unappreciated, and uncared for. She was working at night, full-time, getting very little sleep, and then taking care of the children and doing household chores during the day, all by herself. Subsequent discussion drew out the fact that father was helping quite a lot more than he was given credit for, but he gave his help in such a way that mother felt her mothering role had been usurped. This left her feeling that she had been reduced to simply performing household chores.

It was whilst she was complaining about having to do all the housework by herself that mother demonstrated to me part of the family's underlying difficulties. At the end of the session I watched her crawl around my room on her hands and knees, clearing away the toys with which the children were playing, even though the two little boys had been happily trying to clear the toys by themselves. As she did so, father grabbed Little S from her and placed him close to his chest, but then mother snatched Little S back from him on the way out.

I noticed that there was no pushchair for Little S. Weeks later I learnt that it had been left with friends, and had not been collected since. It seemed to suit the parents not to have the pushchair. It meant that each parent could act out their neediness and desperation to be held and comforted, by vying with one another physically to carry the baby.

Mother felt that she had to work full-time, and at night, because she saw herself as the main breadwinner. Father earned a little less than her, and she used this as the reason for assuming the main breadwinner role. However, his earnings—plus part-time earnings from her—would have been more than adequate for their requirements. It seemed instead that being away from her partner and her children during the night was somehow important to her.

The dilemma for Little S, the so-called 'problem' child, seemed to be how he might be allowed to express his sorrow about the situation in which he found himself—namely, having two distressed parents. How could he obtain comfort in *his* distress? Evidently, crying was not allowed by the parents because of the sadness it aroused in them.

Both children were seeking attention during the session. Older S drew a picture coloured completely black, which he said was a boat, with the letter 'S' next to it. The approaches they made to their parents during the session were ignored. The parents were unable to find a way to accommodate these, because of the strength of their own preoccupations.

The possibility of joint work with the couple was effectively sabotaged by mother taking out a court injunction to prevent father from hitting her. She did this on the day after seeing me for the first time. However, they continued to live together, and I continued to see them. It was my belief that she was the more violent of the pair; the injunction seemed to me about preventing her from hitting him, as much as stopping him from hitting her. Mother seemed to me intent on curing her disturbance by abandoning her partner, which would have resulted in her children sharing her own early life experience—of not having a father.

Meanwhile, Little S was reported to have developed a strange, new behaviour. He began laughing inappropriately whenever his mother looked at him, which frightened her enormously.

The couple brought news that mother's parents were travelling from the Caribbean to the UK on holiday. As this holiday visit approached, I noticed that mother became increasingly persecuted. She took to wearing tinted glasses, as if attempting to block out some of the disturbance she was feeling inside herself. Quarrelling between mother and father reached new heights, partly—I think—because of my own plans to take a holiday. On one occasion mother had to physically move away from father, in order to prevent herself from hitting father with a rolled-up magazine she was carrying. The magazine contained an article on family matters. In the face of mother's extreme aggression, father was forced to reduce his own.

After mother's parents arrived, father observed that mother had become tyrannical. It was evident that she longed for her own mother to treat her as her baby, but instead she was confronted with the reality of her mother's attachment to her stepfather. Mother felt relegated to second place, both by her mother and by me.

The couple held together until my return from holiday. This coincided with the return of mother's stepfather to the Caribbean, although her mother extended her stay in the UK. Tension mounted between the couple when mother moved from the marital bed into her mother's bed—as soon as her stepfather had left a space. Father experienced this as an enormous provocation. They had a violent row, after which the couple separated. Mother went with her mother and the children to a friend's house. She seemed determined to demonstrate to her own mother that she was not a grown-up—that is, that she was not a woman, capable of dealing with a partner, children, a home, and a career.

It was at this point I decided that they should both be seen separately. I continued to see mother, and a colleague saw father. However, father felt rejected by this, and stopped attending sessions.

Mother, meanwhile, simply did not experience the separation from her partner as a true loss—mainly because her own attachments were invested elsewhere. Consciously she would not acknowledge him as possessing any value for her at all; in her mind he was completely incapable of providing her with anything useful, as if he were old rubbish which had to be got rid of. Unconsciously, however, the story was entirely different. She had a dream of *a witch casting a spell on her, although she did not know what the spell was.* In another dream, *she gave father a ten-pence piece, which he swallowed. It stuck in his throat and he vomited out greenish, bilious stuff.* In these dreams was a recognition of her own internal witch-mother-self, whom she experienced as preventing her from having her own man. By leaving the marital bed to sleep in her own mother's bed, she was not only presenting her partner with something 'hard to swallow', she was also dealing with what 'stuck in her own throat'—the fact that her mother and her therapists both had partners, with whom she felt in competition.

A second piece of acting-out particularly intrigued me. Mother went to the flat she had lived in prior to living with father, which she had since rented out to tenants. She then proceeded to attempt to throw out the current occupants, and to install her mother, her children, and herself. Evidently, she and her mother were to be 'the new couple'. When we explored together the meaning of her actions, she reported a feeling of going mad. To me it seemed she was saying that if she were not allowed to take this course of action, then she *would* go mad.

Her rage towards father did not abate as our work progressed, and she entered a state I would describe as 'lost'. She felt unable to take back the care of her children from her mother, and began to hatch plans for her mother to take them back to the Caribbean. I understood this as an expression of her wish to continue to be a child, to continue to be cared for by her mother—through her children—and never have to separate. Meanwhile, father took steps through the Courts to prevent their children from being taken abroad, and also established arrangements for access.

Father's use of the law contributed to jerking mother back into the real world. Her own mother returned home—without the children—and she regained some of her adult self. She rented accommodation for herself and the children, and successfully defeated father's application for custody of the children. She started to drive her own car, whereas previously she had refused to do this and had insisted upon being driven. She then made day-care arrangements for Little S, acquired a new pushchair, and then took up daytime employment.

Little S made a recovery, but then his mother's feelings of persecution began to focus more upon Older S. (Not for the first time, I noted how clients with difficulties concerning separation and individuation seem disposed to give their children names beginning with the same letter.) Mother began to feel attacked by her children's demands—although these were quite ordinary—and retaliated against them verbally. Also, on many occasions, she seemed to be inviting me to attack her parenting of the children.

The gap between being offered care from myself, yet never feeling adequately cared for, instilled in her a deep sense of grievance. It was what she did in her own mind with the care she was offered which formed the crux of the problem. Sometimes she felt understood, in which case she seemed better able to care for her children. When she felt misunderstood, however, she seemed unable to find the means to care for them or for herself.

When I took holidays—especially—she experienced me as a sadistic parental figure, and unconsciously communicated that if I was not going to take care of her then she was not going to take care of her children. It was important at this time—whilst she was acting-out—that she consistently failed to provoke me into berating her and intervening in the care of Little S. In this way we succeeded in talking and thinking about what was happening, rather than becoming embroiled in acting-out together, which would have avoided confrontation of issues which were both painful and potentially explosive.

In a later session she finally recognised her own longing that the child in her be cared for and wanted. On this occasion she arrived fifteen minutes late, without the pushchair, and experienced her usual difficulty with starting to speak. She began by requesting that the sessions be changed to once a fortnight, rather than once a week, on the grounds that she was too busy to come. Another reason she gave was that she did not know what to say when she arrived. My comment was that I thought it felt difficult when she came, and that she would rather be busy in order to avoid feeling uncomfortable. She replied it felt fine, but I could see she was holding back tears. After a period of silence I said it seemed she was feeling upset, and that she looked as if she wanted to cry. Her head bowed, and she put a finger in her mouth in a very baby-like way. She peered up at me from this bowed position, as if to check that I was interested in what she was saying. With what appeared to me a massive effort, she told me that she had been filling in an application form for a job, and that this had made her late. She feared she would not be given the job if she indicated she had children and, when she reached a part of the form which asked her this very question, she did not know whether to answer it truthfully. My interpretation was that she was unconsciously in touch with the child-like parts of herself, which were causing her trouble, and were unacceptable to other people—including myself.

She proceeded to tell me that she wasted my time whenever she came—in fact, the only occasions on which she felt she was not taking up someone else's time were when she was working—but then she went on to talk about not having enough time to do what she wanted to do. I said to her that I thought this indicated a wish for more—rather than less—sessions with me. When I gave her notice that I would be taking a week's holiday, she gave me notice that she would be taking a week off on my return.

Another separation-reaction took the form of a displacement of anger meant for me onto her ex-partner. She spoke of her belief that he was ruining all her best efforts and plans for caring for the children. In her mind, however, it was I who was ruining her plans to ensure the child-like parts of herself were taken care of. She then spoke of her disappointment at the unwillingness of people to help take care of her children on Saturdays, so that she could work. This extra employment would have helped her earn more money. I switched into 'outer world thinking' with her, and we soon discovered that after paying the child-minder she would be no better off financially. Then I returned to the internal issue, which was that she wanted to work with *me* on Saturdays (during *my* free time), in order to increase her inner resources. She wanted to co-operate in the work, but was repeatedly frustrated by what she experienced as my absence. When I was not physically present for her I turned 'bad' in her mind; I was then flung out of her mind and experienced as an absence. She perceived me as always insisting on higher standards of care for her children than she could manage, whilst at the same time I was deserting her and therefore refusing to live up to the standards I myself had set.

When she felt properly 'held' by me, she was more able to hold her thoughts and prevent herself from rushing straight into the mode of action. My physical presence offered her a fresh opportunity to work through the problems she had with maintaining a good object. Her aggressive feelings, and anything which thwarted her wish to control, quickly turned her objects from 'nice' to 'nasty'. However, she was repeatedly confronted by the fact of my separateness from her, just as she had come up against the fact of her separateness from her mother and her partner. This made her feel extremely lonely.

An exploration of her early childhood and adolescence illuminated why this was the case. Her parents had not married. Her mother had taken her baby to bed with her until she had started a new relationship—at which point the baby was simply removed. Her mother married this second partner, and then other babies began to arrive. As the eldest, she felt thoroughly displaced. She recognised this at a deep level, and it was these feelings which had prompted her to prevent her son, Little S, from developing a dependency, which she believed would prove as harmful to him as it had to her.

It was her unconscious knowledge of her own suffering through dependency which had made her inappropriately attempt to curb Little S's dependence upon herself. She wanted him 'toughened up', even before he had had an experience of normal dependence upon his mother. Her own problems with separateness—with which, it seems, her mother and stepfather had been unable to help her—had made it difficult for her to distinguish between her own baby-like needs, and the needs of her real baby.

Her distress had become acute after Little S was born. The birth of this second child may have seemed to her a recurrence of what had happened to herself after her first sibling was born. She was intensely jealous of her partner's close relationship with Little S—as she must have been of her own mother and stepfather's love of her sibling. She felt resentment at having had no father of her own, and—consequently—sought to deprive her own children of fathers also.

However, Little S's mother did make progress within herself, which enabled her to hold me in her mind, preventing her from feeling so lonely. She began to understand her children's needs a little better, and then to share her care of them with their father.

* * *

The mother and father of Little S demonstrate how it sometimes comes about that men and women of Caribbean background sometimes end up living separately, with the men complaining about the women and the women complaining about the men. What seems fairly certain is that there could be no possibility of harmony whilst mother persisted in her attempts to be the child in her own mother's bed. There are many different ways of understanding this desire, depending upon one's theoretical position. In Freudian terms, most definitely she had not succeeded in negotiating the Oedipus complex. And she certainly was not helped to do so by a mother who unconsciously colluded with her wishes to attack men—both her partner, and her stepfather. However, mother's own mother may have been acutely aware of her daughter's distress, and may have been attempting to help her daughter cope with it in the only way she knew how.

Little S's father, on the other hand, had been married previously, and had older children who remained with their mother at the time of their parents' divorce. Father had been anxious to make a success of the new relationship, and of parenting both his son and his stepson. He was hindered, however, by his own lack of experience of having been fathered. He knew about mothering, but not about fathering. His own mother had raised her children single-handedly, and was reportedly keen to teach him how to look after himself without the need of any other women.

Father—rightly—felt cheated of receiving care from me. As I mentioned, he abandoned his sessions with a colleague of mine, and left feeling very hurt. Defeated by these failures in his relationships to women—which he was unable to understand—he threatened to have nothing more to do with them. At the time, I did not appreciate the formidable struggle which confronts men of Caribbean origin in maintaining their places—not only their positions as partners, husbands, and fathers, but also as clients and patients. In retrospect I now recognise that Little S's mother and father should have been provided with two workers from the very beginning of the treatment.

Chapter Nine

A Feeling of 'Not Belonging'

A feeling of not belonging can arise in any adult, but seems to be especially prevalent and acute among people who have been trans-racially adopted, or who are sent away to boarding school very early in their lives. However, slavery can also produce this feeling in people, because it creates a paradox: you belong to the owner, and yet—at the same time—you do not belong anywhere.

In the Caribbean, there has always been a system of informal adoption—that is, adoption by private arrangement, between family or friends, without the intervention of the State. There is no doubt that some children have benefited greatly from this system. Even so, the breaking of *all* ties with the natural parents, which became the hallmark of the 'permanency movement' of the 1980s,[17] seems to me to have been very unfortunate. Total severance of relations with the natural parents creates unnecessary conflict in the children, as well as a sense of permanent separation, and of broken relationships which are impossible to mend. In the 1990s there has been another shift away from the breakage of ties, towards a maintenance of relationships with the natural parents.

* * *

M was trans-racially adopted. Her natural parents originated from two different Caribbean countries, whereas her adoptive parents were a white British couple who already had two children of their own. M seemed on the outside successful and well-adjusted, but felt every bit as homeless as might a child discharged from a children's home who is forced to live on the streets.

M's natural mother migrated to Britain from the Caribbean when she was a small child, the youngest in her family. The father of M's mother dies during her childhood, and partly as a consequence of this—it appeared—M's mother was dominated by her own mother. My understanding of the situation is that M's mother started a relationship with M's father, became pregnant, and that M's father wished to marry her. However, under pressure from her own mother, M's mother decided to continue her education, refused the offer of marriage, and gave the baby up for adoption. It was unusual for black women from this type of background, at this time, to give up their babies for adoption. However, what seems on the surface to have been a case of a mother harbouring ambitions for her daughter, would probably have revealed—upon closer inspection—a frightened woman without a husband, in a new country, effectively hanging onto her daughter in order to use her as a substitute partner. M's mother did manage to leave home some years later and marry another man. However, there were no children from this marriage and it did not last.

* * *

M's adoptive mother had trained in the performing arts, and had hoped to pursue a career in this field, but although she was talented she lacked the confidence needed to perform.

M's adoptive father was the younger of two sons. His own father had died when he was two years old. He had been sent to boarding school early in life, and had achieved highly academically. Of her adoptive parents M once commented: 'I don't think Mum would have had me. It was father's side of the family who felt guilty about the poor'. This revealed how unvalued she felt.

As a new-born infant, M was passed from her natural mother to foster parents. At six months her adoptive parents received her. By the time legal formalities were completed, M was already nine-months-old and had experienced a lot of disruption in her short life. More was to follow. Her new parents immediately left M and their two older children with the paternal grandfather, whilst they went on a month's holiday abroad. When M was one-year-old, she experienced more disruption when the family moved house. They moved again when she was four, and yet again when she was five. The early relocations—from one pair of arms to another, from one house to another—left their mark on her. In later life she felt 'unable to settle'. I suspect that it was not only the moves themselves which caused her trouble, but also the way in which they were handled.

When M was five-years-old she found herself with even more to cope with: an older cousin, a girl on the maternal side whose mother had died, also came to live with the family. This helped M in a way, as the cousin assisted in taking care of her, until M was ten, at which time the cousin—then a teenager—left the family after a serious row with father. M was deeply upset by the loss of this close friend.

When M was eleven, her father gave up his well-paid job and bought a smallholding, onto which the family moved. The paternal grandmother moved in with them. The parents found themselves very busy, looking after the smallholding and the grandmother. M's mother also did part-time work. When M moved into this latest home she lost the few friends she had managed to make at school since the last move. She met no-one who was the same colour as herself during her entire childhood, and was always the only black child in the area for miles around, wherever they lived. This made her feel isolated, and deprived of friends and peers. Her parents were sufficiently concerned by her isolation to join a multi-racial social group. However, M hid from the only African couple which came to visit. With no friends of her own she tended to follow around her brothers and their friends.

M became a very angry and rebellious adolescent. At fourteen she was sexually active—initially with one of her brother's friends. She sided with her brother in rebellious confrontations with their father, and often stayed out late. She was not usually collected from evening activities, and there seemed to be a particular lack of concern from her mother. Her relationship with her father was quarrelsome—to say the least—but he did notice her. They argued over wastage of water (which was a precious resource on the smallholding) which she used for bathing, in order to keep herself cool, because by this time she was suffering from eczema which had broken out all over her body. She must have felt dirty, in every sense of the word. She was also drinking heavily by the age of fourteen, but this too was ignored by her parents.

When she was fifteen, her father became so angry with her one day that he took her to a forest, and left her there. She hitched a lift home, but mother refused to let her in for fear of upsetting father. She was forced to spend the night at the home of the only adult she felt able to ask for help: a local male shop-keeper. Even so, she felt in danger of being sexually abused by him. The following day her mother collected her and took her home. About a year later, at the age of sixteen, in a desperate bid for independence she moved out of the family home and into a bed-sit. Soon after she left the paternal grandmother died, and within a few months the father had a breakdown.

* * *

M's perception of these events was that things had been going badly wrong in the family for a long time, but that her parents had not sought any help for her because she was adopted. However, one of their natural children had also experienced trouble—with the police.

M had arrived at the belief that it was she herself who had instigated the plan for the family to buy the smallholding. She also felt that she did more than her fair share of the work involved in running it. 'I worked harder than anyone else, but it was not appreciated', she told me. 'When I left they stopped keeping cows and pigs'.

The lack of protection, caring and control in M's upbringing led me to wonder whether there was a connection with the lack of care evident in her parents' own childhoods, and with their need to adopt a black child in particular.

As a family they seemed socially isolated. This isolation was not caused by their adoption of a black child—although this may have exacerbated it—but instead by a more run-of-the-mill difficulty connected with getting along with people in general. The presence of a black child in this white family may have given them a *reason* for isolation, but it was certainly not the cause of it. The family's retreat to the smallholding seems to have been a 'psychotic' manoeuvre, which further isolated them. As I mentioned, M felt that she herself was implicated in the acquisition of the farm. I suggested this was because she herself was the family's 'small holding'—that is, a child to hold them together.

On leaving home, in identification with her mother, M took a job as an entertainer. Given her background, I was not surprised to hear that the first man with whom she formed a relationship at this time physically abused her. However, she had a better experience with a second boyfriend who encouraged her to finish her education. She became very depressed and unhappy at this point, and made her first attempt at suicide by taking an overdose of pills. With her boyfriend's help she started work with a white counsellor, but left very soon on the grounds that the counsellor 'was not the right colour'. M, it seemed, was in search of the 'right' mother.

She completed her studies and moved into the adult world of work, where she acted-out her difficulties surrounding who she was and with whom she belonged by moving backwards and forwards between rival theatre companies. In her mind the companies were 'black' and 'white' in a very concrete sense. It is interesting to note how social and political arrangements to separate 'ethnic' from 'mainstream' facilitate the psychopathology of the individuals involved. The rival theatre companies which M moved between placed themselves precisely in one or other of these two discrete camps.

The precipitating factor which brought her to therapy was disturbance following her first sexual encounter with a black man. She felt angry with him when he wanted nothing further to do with her. She felt he had abused her, and she tried to have him punished. When her attempts failed she became seriously depressed. This led her to return to her adoptive parents, and to ask for their help in tracing her natural mother.

* * *

M dressed in a sexually provocative way for her first consultation with me, and decided not to take up therapy. A year later, however, she returned for a second consultation. In the intervening year she had found her natural mother, but was very disappointed with her. M felt also that her adoptive parents had displaced her, and that they took more notice of the newly rediscovered natural mother than of their adoptive daughter. This hurt her deeply and made her very bitter. She made no efforts to find her natural father.

For the second consultation M presented herself dressed as a little girl, with her natural hair tied in two bunches. She talked of her worry about her inability to settle anywhere, and about how she could not commit herself to a relationship with the man with whom she was living. She was bulimic and drinking heavily. This time she decided to start therapy.

M came once a week, and was unable to commit herself to more sessions. She began therapy on the couch, placing herself the wrong way around with her head at the foot of the couch — a communication of how she felt. Perhaps she wanted to see my face, and to have me hold her feet in order to prevent her from running away. She placed my cushions on the floor, and told me—later—that she had stopped using pillows after she visited Africa and discovered there were no pillows whatsoever in the village in which she stayed. I felt she was implying she had no African mother's breasts on which to rest her head—a reference, then, to the natural mother she had discovered the previous year. She not only refused my cushions but wanted to trample them, and often managed to kick them accidentally.

Her underlying fear, at the start of therapy, was of being abused and of abusing me. The early sessions were almost totally silent. I came to distinguish an alternation between silent tearful sorrow (which flowed outwards), and silent screaming tears (which she would swallow). She found it impossible to put her thoughts into words and to share them—an indication of the pre-verbal origin of her difficulties.

She very much needed my help to 'bring her into' the sessions, and I soon learnt very directly about how she must have been a small child who spent many sleepless nights quietly alone in her room. She had never slept well, and had sometimes left her bed to play with her toys during the night, or she would wander about the house on her own. Her parents would put her back into bed with a hot drink. From these experiences she must have learnt that drinks are the appropriate treatment for distress, rather than talking. She seemed to have searched continually for a mother who might receive her worried communications, and on whose breast she might fall asleep peacefully. In therapy she continued to be the child who looked after herself; a child who earned her keep, but who was not liked because of her colour.

As she settled into therapy, the corpse-like person on the couch began to show some signs of life. Loving concern seemed quite unknown to her. My interpretations were perceived as forcing something unwanted into her. Her response was to become totally mute, which was her means of protecting me from abuse and herself from what she experienced as intrusiveness. She wanted no intervention from me.

The first holiday break gave her proof of my criminality. To her I was an abandoning parent. After the break, however, things took a turn for the better. She increased her sessions to thrice-weekly and the cushions were elevated from the floor to the chair. She took responsibility for coming to see me, whereas before her partner had brought her.

Questions were raised which had to do with forming a couple. Could she and myself form a couple? Did I value her? Could we value each other, or was she a hopeless case? She was very sensitive about her appearance—especially concerning what she perceived as her imperfect hair. She wanted hair like her adoptive mother. 'My hair extensions are my chains', she told me. 'Most girls with plaits are confused. I won't be liked if I don't wear them. Women who wear their hair naturally are a threat; they are not afraid.' She both envied and feared me, much as she had feared the African visitors. She also envied black people their 'deprivation', and had great difficulty in perceiving black people as anything other than 'deprived people'. In this respect, I think she probably identified with her parents and with most white people. This seems to be a common problem for trans-racially adopted black children.

Even within herself there was no place she felt comfortable. She lived in a state of fear, as if she were about to be found out and exposed for not being herself. This was expressed, at first, in terms of colour. She told me that in the company of white people she felt small: 'Sometimes I feel so small I don't exist; I don't have the right to speak up'. She was embarrassed when her white colleagues found she did not understand the street-talk of 'inner city' young black people. She was totally crushed when a white colleague remarked to her: 'You're more white than me'. She stated she felt like a bridge that was continually walked over. For her, being 'walked over' was what being black was all about. Hers was a world divided into 'top' and 'bottom'.

As the therapy continued, the difficulty concerning her sense of belonging expressed itself less in terms of colour ('whites versus blacks') but increasingly in terms of which set of black people she might join. The underlying question was whether I could be trusted; whether she could join up with the 'black mother' part of her therapist. She herself was still stuck in the position of a deprived infant, feeling 'little' inside herself and in the company of others. In the sessions it was clear she felt she was being offered accommodation by me, but was struggling to accept it. She informed me that a (white) friend had offered her a vacant flat, but that the friend's boyfriend did not want her to move in. This was a reference to myself, split into an 'accommodating' part, as well as a part that did not like her because of her colour. This suggests an internal state of affairs in which mothers in general—black and white—did not like her, which suggests that she was not in contact with her *own* ambivalence towards them.

Her ambivalence towards me, meanwhile, was set to continue. On one occasion she ridiculed my interpretation that she was missing me and that she wanted me to cook dinner for her. After mocking me, however, she would become depressed. She continued to become progressively involved with me even though—outwardly—she denied all need of me. She wanted to co-operate with me, but her anger prevented her from enjoying a loving intercourse with me. There was a question in her mind over whether we could tolerate success: whether she could tolerate my success with her, and whether I could tolerate her success outside the sessions. I linked this to what she perceived as her adoptive mother's lack of success in her upbringing.

The announcement of my next holiday break again fed into her early experiences of being repeatedly taken up and put down. She responded by announcing holiday dates of her own, and—later that same week—dreamt that she was murdering her partner. She interpreted my forthcoming absence as an overt lack of respect for her feelings. It was clear she felt she had been dropped yet again, and was in danger of splintering into bits. It seemed she was held together only by murderous anger.

In her mind I was a mother who had committed the crime of giving her up as a baby and then forgetting all about her. By going on holiday I was now repeating this crime. I was unable to interest her in the idea of continuing to work with someone who had a 'criminal record', but who—although 're-offending' by leaving her physically—would not be abandoning her psychically over the break. She responded to this by sleeping through an entire session. This was 'acting-in'! Although the thought of separation was intolerable, she had given up on me, and resumed an abusive relationship with a man she described as a 'Rastafarian'. She seemed to be making every effort to revenge herself on me by retreating into shamefulness. As she flung me aside, because I was someone who might care for her and help her think things through, she became very muddled, sometimes arriving late, or up to an hour early, or sometimes not showing up at all. When she did turn up for these final sessions before the break, she would have nothing to do with me. She arrived for her last session before the holiday smelling of drink. Her addiction to despair was complete, and the therapy was being systematically destroyed.

* * *

M did not attend her first session after the break. She contacted me by telephone, to let me know that she had moved from her friend's flat and had left her job. This was followed by a series of calls, from many different parts of the country, which I was asked to return. She was not available to receive any of my replies. She was behaving extremely provocatively, and made every effort to make it difficult for me to communicate with her in a meaningful way.

Looking back now, I can understand this as a way of making me experience what it had felt like for her, as the worried baby passed from one pair of arms to another. Speaking with her on the telephone, I failed to recognise this and so did not put it to her. Later she made a request—also by telephone—that I find her somewhere to live, because she was homeless. I interpreted this (again, by phone) as her wish that I adopt her. However, I now think that she was actually asking the reverse: she was putting me in the position of the mother who sent her away for adoption.

By catching hold of at least some of the underlying issues, it seemed I succeeded in bringing her back to therapy. She returned after several weeks, looking like a derelict and in an attacking frame of mind. She announced that she had set up appointments with two new therapists offering treatments for her various symptoms. She believed they would deal with the problems she had originally presented in a more practical way. She rubbished the work we had done and, taking from her bag a book called *The Deadly Diet*, invited me to discard my form of therapy in favour of the one she had discovered in the book. I interpreted this as her wish to convince me that I could not help her, that I was useless, and that no-one could help her. I also took up with her the significance of the 'deadly diet' (her bulimia) on which she had put herself. She left the session in a state of ambivalence over whether she should continue with therapy, but within an hour of arriving home she telephoned me, and asked to start again. Two days later, however, she phoned again, this time to change her mind. She had decided to give the two new therapists a try, adding that she might contact me again in the future. It seemed to me that the new therapists stood for her adoptive parents.

M's wound was too raw for her to tolerate being taken up and put down, at the time of the holiday break. This played havoc with her emotional digestive system, causing a resurgence of her bulimia. She needed to be rid of me, and so she vomited me out.

The therapy helped her to begin to think a little, and to put into words some of her painful early experiences. It also enabled her to begin to separate from herself both sets of her parents, and to begin to discover that she had a self. However, this self was the 'bridge which people walked over'. She was identified with being a victim and, to her, all black people were in the same position. She found it difficult to find another way of being. She could not belong because, to her, to belong was to be abused. I, by being black, was both an affront to her convictions, and a provocation of her envy.

She had the capacity to feed from me; in fact, she was a 'secret feeder', with enormous hunger. She wanted, it seemed, an experience she had never enjoyed in reality—of taking hold of the breast, possessing it, and hanging onto it until she felt full and content, and then of falling asleep on the breast, and of waking up and finding her mother still present. A holiday break was a frustration she simply could not tolerate. If I was not going to keep her—as she perceived it—it was because I was ashamed of her. In return, she would shame me by her behaviour, feeding instead from the abusive so-called 'Rastafarian'.

Her early life experiences had complicated the ordinary difficulty of joining up the good and bad parts of her object, and had left her with strong feelings of ambivalence. Her 'black self' began to emerge as she learnt to differentiate between black people. In therapy she became acquainted for the first time with the notion that being black was not a disaster. The healthy part of her fragile black self experienced great trouble in connecting with me; I became a black (and a white) persecutor, who deprived her of good things. Her frustration, at feeling she was offered only rubbish for food, produced anger. She set off to find a new diet for herself, over which (through bulimia) she would have total control.

Having two sets of parents is difficult for anyone, but having also to confront in adolescence two sets of parents from different ethnic backgrounds, who could never come together in her mind in a positive way (due to the lack of a society which can be considered multiracial in a deep sense), was bound to cause trouble in a young woman already so internally frail. Her rebelliousness, expressed through bulimia, was the result of early neglect which had been internalised. As far as she was concerned, to be black—that is, different from her adoptive parents—was a disaster. This was how she imagined every black person felt about themselves. When she began to question this assumption she also began to find a black self of worth, around which she could begin to build a better sense of self in general.

She was correct in thinking that the task of growing and accepting herself as a black woman was made more difficult by her trans-racial adoption. Her main trouble as an adult, however, was with accepting personal responsibility for her own hatred of herself. I think that a therapist of any colour would have had to confront her problem over making good use of a therapist. She stayed with me for longer than she had with a previous therapist, but left before completing the treatment, although with a warning that she might return. She wanted the door left open for her, which I read as an indication that she did sense the possibility of belonging.

M chose to take her symptoms elsewhere for treatment, as an alternative to uncovering the whole of the troubled, infantile part of herself. She decided she did not want to learn about how to take care of this part, and about how she might eventually take responsibility for her own care—which could have helped her feel that she belonged. By abandoning me she may also have been paying back her natural mother for the crime of giving her up for adoption. Her natural mother had not allowed her to belong, and her adoptive parents had failed in making her feel that she belonged. By leaving therapy she sought to save herself from unbearable pain, and from having to receive anything or be grateful to anyone, which might have led her to feel suicidally depressed.

* * *

Two additional tragedies were uncovered by our work together. The first is the tragedy of M's natural mother—a young woman utterly trapped by her own mother, who herself had been unable to cope with the loss of her husband, her country, and support from her extended family. M's natural mother was unable to find a way of joining with her boyfriend, becoming a wife and a mother to M. M's natural father, meanwhile, was eliminated from the picture altogether, but must have haunted M through the figure of the black man with whom she had a brief relationship, who had abandoned her and whom she wanted to punish. M's grandmother (for whom M reserved a particular hatred) had passed on to M's mother the need to become a successful breadwinner rather than a successful wife and mother. As I have argued, this is the legacy of a culture based on slavery, in which men were perceived as unable to support women.

The second tragedy which our work uncovered was that of M's adoptive father, who also seemed trapped in resentment towards his mother. He was a successful man, in many respects, yet he was dogged by unresolved difficulties from his earliest childhood, which he seems to have sought to remedy by adopting M. As a young boy without a father, separated very early from his mother, he must have felt completely abandoned. His motivation for the adoption was to demonstrate to his mother that he could be a better parent than she had been to him. M's adoptive mother, equally, may have needed an object into which she could project unwanted parts of herself. But of course, there are no perfect parents, adoptive or natural.

Matching parents and children of the same race may work well in adoption and fostering, but it is not necessarily a good idea in the context of the relationship between patient and therapist. The role of therapist is of course very different from the role of parent. However, the level at which M's difficulties were situated was such that she did appear to require the reality of a black psychotherapist, in order to work-through some of the muddle which surrounded black people in her mind. Feelings of being unloved, unrespected, can easily become projected onto race. M had developed a mind-set according to which all white people were privileged, and all black people deprived victims. I felt it was important to use the reality of a black ther-

Chapter Ten

On 'Struggle'

The term 'struggle' is very much a part of the vocabulary of British Caribbean people. Although there are many social, political, and personal definitions of 'struggle', for the most part it is understood as referring to something which occurs between the individual and his or her outside world.

To my mind, 'struggle' is best understood as the refusal of a non-frustrating object—that is, as the rejection, by a person, of any object which might provide that person with satisfaction. In other words, 'to struggle' is to set oneself wilfully in direct opposition to ease and freedom. The circumstances which can lead a person to reject what might otherwise provide them with satisfaction will differ in each case. In my opinion, however, emotional deprivation, coupled with severe frustration from the external world, seem to be at the heart of all forms of struggle.

Because the person engaged in struggle *chooses* to reject satisfaction, this leads to a characteristic attitude of 'acceptance' of suffering and distress. During slavery, for instance, this 'acceptance' of suffering, this determination to struggle, was adopted with the simple aim of survival.

I hope to illustrate some of these themes, as they appeared in the treatment and early life of a patient, whose commitment to struggle is explored below.

* * *

E came for psychotherapy at the suggestion of a friend. To the friend it seemed obvious that E needed professional help, whereas it had not occurred to E herself that she ought to seek assistance. Her presenting problem was dissatisfaction with her work situation, which she experienced as abusive. She also felt angry with her husband for failing to remove and protect her from the stresses of her everyday world.

E's parents came from different social backgrounds from within the same Caribbean country. Her father had arrived in the UK to join family members who had already settled. He met and married E's mother soon after her arrival in the UK. E was the couple's first child. Unlike her husband, E's mother had no family in the UK.

As an infant of six weeks, E had been sent away to foster parents, because her mother was unable to look after her. The parents felt that there was no room for a baby in their extremely cramped living conditions. To me it seemed that E's mother had been afraid that her own mental health would suffer if she stayed at home with the baby, in the extremely reduced circumstances in which she found herself. However, given that many other Caribbean mothers kept their babies despite having to endure similar circumstances, I was led to conclude that E's mother, without the support of her own mother or family, simply could not find the internal resources necessary to hold onto her child.

E's mother returned to work after the birth, but—although she was never hospitalised—was considered sufficiently unwell to have been referred to a psychiatrist. I think this was mostly due to her evident inability to adapt to the harshness of her life, for which she had received no preparation. In the Caribbean it would have been more likely that someone would have helped her to take care of a first child—such as a maternal grandmother, for instance. In the UK, however, the early migrants lived in a socially inhospitable climate. Sometimes they would have to make stark choices between either caring for their children by themselves, or putting a roof over their heads. Frequently they would loose both home and children, as a consequence of disruption to the bond between parents and children, and of governmental redevelopment policies. Having grown up in societies with a history of women working equally hard alongside men, these British Caribbean mothers set about making work a priority in their lives. Welfare was frowned upon by people used to fending entirely for themselves.

E was somewhat confused about the details of her early life. To begin with, she told me that she had spent her first five years with foster parents. As time went on, however, I learnt that she went home to her natural parents at week-ends, and returned to live with them permanently when she was two-years-old. By this time her parents had bought a house.

She grew up with the idea that people were not to be trusted. Her mother had two sayings, which had remained with E throughout her life. These were: 'People are envious of you', and: 'People don't want to see you do well'. This lack of trust in the goodwill of others seems to have been rooted in E's mother's distrust of her own mother.

E began seeing me twice weekly, but took up the offer a third session within weeks of commencing therapy. She appeared to be a co-operative patient. She attended on time and never missed sessions. She appeared genuinely to want to come, and apparently appreciated the space set aside for her, but nevertheless had a real difficulty with developing any trust in me. After eighteen months she still had trouble acknowledging that she needed help from me. She seemed to need to protect what she had by keeping it secret, because she was afraid it would be taken away from her.

Her resistance to working with me finally broke through in the following way, just one week before the holiday break. She arrived for her session stating that she was extremely tired. She had slept only three hours the previous night, because she had stayed up to complete some work which—she claimed—had to be submitted before her own holiday, which also began the following week.

To me it seemed tidying up work in her external world was a way in which her internal world (her mind) would also become tidy, and she would then be able to feel rested during the break. She went on to say that she could only work under pressure, otherwise she felt a tendency to procrastinate. She would attend to innumerable other tasks rather than the one she knew was most important. Her 'three hours sleep' was a reference to her three sessions; and her wakefulness was a reference to her attempts to give herself therapy, without needing my help.

Next, however, she recalled a phonecall she had received from a colleague the day before. The phonecall had made her very angry. Her colleague had enquired how she was progressing with an important piece of work which E knew she had been putting off. E felt under pressure after ending the call, and had sworn at the caller after putting down the phone. It became apparent that the pressure she felt originated from inside herself, rather than from outside. The colleague had, in fact, not been demanding immediate completion of the work, even though E evidently experienced a great deal of discomfort after being reminded that she had not yet tackled it.

E seemed to be having difficulty differentiating between inside and outside. I pointed out her muddle over whether the pressure was coming from within or without herself. I suggested that she felt under pressure to complete the work of therapy all by herself before we stopped for the break. Her response to this was to fall into an angry silence.

After a while she spoke again. She remembered a similar feeling as a schoolgirl when a teacher (who also acted as her careers tutor) had not wanted her to do well. The teacher had been reluctant to put E forward to take an O Level examination, but had suggested that she took the (lower level) CSE examination instead. The teacher had agreed with E that her work was good when she managed to complete it, but that this always seemed to involve a terrible struggle, rooted in E's ambivalence towards her work. The teacher (whom E described as a 'colonial type') had tried to persuade her against taking up this struggle, but E had insisted that she be allowed to continue. With enormous effort she passed the O Level examination, and felt triumphant. She had shown the teacher that she could succeed.

In her therapy, then, at an unconscious level, she was really very disappointed in me (the colonial type), and her disappointment was perceived even more acutely because of the holiday break. Rather than taking her through the work which she knew had to be done, and which she knew she had been putting off, instead I was going away. I was the 'colonial' mother who ruled over her, abandoning her with no respect for her feelings and needs. Although she had had no words with which to remember her experience as an infant, those feelings were now recurring in therapy with me, as they had with the teacher when E had been a schoolgirl.

From the telephone conversation with her colleague, it seemed that E was readily in contact with a negative presence, a bad object, inside herself. What she heard from this part of herself was that she could not do her job, and it was this message which generated in her enough anger to fuel her to produce the work. Completing the work, then, was not something achieved between a co-operative pair (she and myself), or between co-operating parts of herself, but in the context of a battle between herself, the colleague (myself, in the transference), and the work. She triumphed again only after a night of hard toil, except this time she was able to say to me that what she was doing was 'mad', and that she was troubled by it.

However, the enjoyment of all triumphs is short-lived; she was aware that she was unable to complete and enjoy her work for its own sake. The essence of the difficulty lay in admitting to herself that she had any need of help from me (the mother, the teacher). She struggled alone, because—having been let down so badly in her early life—she could not take the risk of allowing this to happen to her again.

E was expected to do well at school on behalf of the whole family. Their status depended upon her. E's mother, after migrating to the UK, had not been unable to complete her education and take up a professional career. E's father, meanwhile, was an intelligent, but uneducated, man from a rural background. E's mother, then, had endured a drop in her social status, and had finally taken a job well below her abilities. E had the idea that her mother would not tolerate failure from her daughter, although she might accept this from a son. Father, however, was much more accepting of E on her own terms. Yet, in order to maintain her place in her mother's esteem, E believed she had to work hard at school, and was unable to find any means of expressing to her mother that she found the work extremely difficult.

E's foster family—a white family, with many children—seem to have provided her with a loving environment. When E returned to her natural parents she encountered a new baby—her brother. Contact with the foster family was eventually lost. The hurt of these early separations from her natural parents and her foster family was never acknowledged. This, plus having to come to terms with a sibling who had the attentions of their mother to himself, contributed to the development of a morass of angry feelings inside E. However, open expression of this anger and distress would have been psychically extremely dangerous and life-threatening to E. A pattern developed of keeping these feelings inside and of not trusting others. As we have seen, this emotional constellation is very similar to that which perpetuated itself through generations of people who suffered the effects of slavery.

E's internal morass of discontent consisted of extremely resentful and angry responses to any demands that she please others—particularly mother-figures. She also felt deeply ambivalent when it came to completing tasks, because of what she perceived as a lack of acknowledgement of her personal worth. To complete a task led to expectations of envy and deflation. 'If I had had your opportunities', her mother would comment, 'I could have done well also'. E felt persecuted by the anticipation of her mother's coldness—the lack of warmth and praise—yet she simultaneously felt guilty for hating her mother over this, as well as feeling sad for herself at becoming so stuck in these feelings.

With her mind filled up in this way E could not move forward. Although she deeply wanted to be able to complete her work, she knew perfectly well that she would still feel no joy in its completion. In this case, there seemed little point in finishing it at all, so the avoidance had to be carried on for hour after hour, and—in this way—the aggressive feelings she experienced towards me could be held in check, so as to preserve her place in my (and her mother's) regard. This also kept her own mind intact and avoided fragmentation.

This arrangement was indeed a form of 'enslavement', which she perceived as being imposed upon her from outside. It was other people who were preventing her from achieving her goals. 'Other' people, in this case, took the shape of white people ('colonial types'), and mothers without feelings for babies (her therapist foremost among them). She was enslaved by negative parts of herself which were profoundly suspicious of others, and deeply unforgiving.

The conflict between caring for children and earning money was being passed on through the generations of E's family. I learnt that E's maternal grandmother had had a job which took her away from her children. The sense of distrust of others which E's mother passed on to E, therefore, was rooted in actual experiences of not being able to rely on mother for adequate care. Economic conditions at the time perhaps influenced these patterns, but I am sure they were not the whole story. There are always people who, despite abject poverty, are nevertheless capable of making their babies feel loved and valued.

The very early experience for E of being separated from her mother, and her mother's subsequent ill health, resulted in feelings of enormous frustration, unhappiness and rage. The unhappiness of E's foster parents—who, at this time, suffered the loss of one of their children—must also have left E prone to depression. She became a child addicted to frustration; a child who habitually refused any object which was non-frustrating. For instance, she would not allow her natural mother to care for her when she returned to her parents' home. She was not able to play naturally, and instead hid herself away by reading books. Later, as an adolescent, she avoided going out with her peers and looked down on what she perceived as their 'frivolity'. She took a part-time job instead of spending time with her friends. Her parents' attitude to money meant that they tended to turn a blind eye to what she was doing.

Although E had received messages from her parents which urged her to beware of the envy of others, she had never confronted her *own* envy. Her therapy puzzled her in this respect. Was I an enemy or a friend? She saw the teacher (myself, in the transference) as protecting her from what the teacher perceived as stress, but this left her feeling unvalued. As E said of herself: 'I was not one of her high flyers'. She was jealous of my other patients—as she had been of her brother—and perceived them also as 'high flyers', having more than she, and doing better. In a sense, it was indeed true that her brother had received more from their mother, and was in better shape.

By releasing her hatred towards her colleague, E was approaching her work in a way based on triumph over the bad object, rather than upon adopting a loving interest in the job to be done. Without enemies, then, E was unable to function at her best; this paranoid structure was essential in order that her feelings of frustration were maintained and her hatred could continue to provide fuel for her work. It was a way of functioning which seemed to be keeping at bay terrible states of depression.

During this very same session, just before the holiday break, E told me that she had not wanted to come that day, because she was afraid to tell me 'the truth' that she had been up for most of the night toiling 'like a mad woman'. She understood that the demand that she work had originated from an internal, tyrannical part of herself (a 'colonial' part of her), which was far more severe than either her own actual parents, or myself. However, as she worked, and as both the morning and the time of the session approached, she seemed to move from the paranoid-schizoid world into a saner realm, in which I was more present and benign, as someone who wanted to help her to feel well and also to do well. Neither myself, nor her colleague, nor the teacher, nor even her mother could safely be blamed, because what was happening to her—she now began to understand—was entirely of her own creation.

The turning point for E might also be described in terms of a turning away from 'lies' towards 'truth'. I became someone who could accept 'the truth' of what she really suffered and really thought about other people, and—more importantly—was someone who could survive this truth and continue to hold her. The truth included her pure hatred, as well as her love. Being able to confront this and speak about it made her feel safer, and—over time—less entangled in the conflict between wanting to please me and not wanting to please me. The idea of pleasing *herself* began to rise towards the forefront. The consequent release of aggression entailed a sudden availability of energy which she could use to complete her work in both her external and internal worlds. Of course, she had been perfectly capable of performing her work all along, but the blockage caused by the neurotic conflict had prevented her from doing this.

As our work progressed, she became able to give up her constant need to construct new enemies against which she had to struggle and triumph. She was able to organise herself to a point at which she decided to change her job, and her anger towards her husband also decreased. This gave her a real taste of personal freedom, satisfaction, and pleasure. She recognised her true enemies for what they were: troublesome parts of herself, projected outwards into the external world.

Chapter Eleven

Childhood Troubles in the Workplace

K approached an educational psychologist, to request a class-room observation of her son, J, and for suggestions on ways she might help J at home. Subsequently her son was seen by the psychologist and a child psychotherapist, and a decision was made to offer him educational therapy.

J made very good use of this opportunity. From having been entirely unable to read, suddenly his interest in books took off. However, in the meantime, K—despite having brought her son to therapy—was now threatening to disrupt the treatment he was receiving, because she was completely unable to trust other people to help J. She simply couldn't understand how it was that she herself could not manage to meet all J's needs.

J's educational therapist expressed an opinion that J needed a protected space to think and to make sense of things for him-self; a place, in other words, in which he might not be intruded upon. It transpired that K herself had been heavily intruded upon by her mother when she was a child, and therefore knew no other way of being with her children.

On this occasion, then, the child guidance team working together with J decided—rightly, in my opinion—to keep their work with the child separate from any work with the parents, although the educational therapist met regularly with both J's parents to discuss his progress. The team had recognised K's envy of her child at the assessment stage, and I was asked to see K for individual therapy. Soon we were meeting regularly, for two sessions a week.

* * *

K was a well-groomed and confident woman. She had a respon-sible job, despite being badly shaken in the recent past by what she described as a series of disasters, which had 'disrupted the smooth-running, happy family life we once had'. To her mind, this sequence of disasters began with her son having nightmares. Things grew worse when her husband was made redundant from his job. Then she had a miscarriage, and began to suffer from severe abdominal pain. The final catastrophe had been her discovery that her son—despite her great hopes for his future—was not learning at school. Previously, she had believed that such things only happened to 'other people', not to her own family. She was very frightened by these developments, but I suspect that the difficulties with her son actually gave her permission to look for some help for herself.

The feelings of fear she brought to the session were of very long standing. She was the second child of her parents, but the first to be born in the UK. Her sister has been left behind with her grandparents—possibly, it seemed to me, as a means of easing K's mother's separation from her own mother. Father had come to the UK first, mother had followed, and then they had married. The couple worked hard, bought their home, and then gave birth to K.

Maya Angelou wrote of black women: 'They knew the burden of feminine sensibilities suffocated by masculine responsibilities... These women have descended from grandmothers and great grandmothers who knew the lash firsthand, and to whom protection was nothing more than an abstraction' (Angelou1998: 42-4). Indeed, it struck me with force that K herself still seemed to possess a knowledge of the lash. She feared being damaged, and also the prospect of doing damage. It was evident that at some level she was aware of the way in which she was intruding upon her son—in the same way her own mother had intruded upon her. Her physical symptoms suggested that she felt damage had been done to the female parts of her own body—in effect, to her femininity.

K had been the child of a mother who had possessed a slaver mentality, a child who still needed to become her own person, by being emancipated. K felt that her mother had not granted her permission to value the maternal role. Instead, she had received the message from her mother that going out to work should be regarded as much more important than staying at home to look after babies. In effect, it was as if K's mother had said to her: 'I left my baby, so you should leave yours too'.

In growing up, then, K became well acquainted with the sensation of *fear*, transmitted to her by the slave-driver parts of her mother. K had a lack of respect for her own individuality; disobedience or questions simply drove mother mad, so there was no space left in K for thinking about the *reasonableness* of particular requests or demands.

It seemed to me that, in common with many mothers newly arrived in this country, K's mother had had trouble becoming fully maternally preoccupied with her baby. Women in this position tended to worry about the children they had left behind, even when they were safe in the hands of other family members. There was often a sense of tremendous guilt about 'abandoning' them, and a terrible sense of loss—for the mothers in particular. This affected their ability to experience any joy in their new babies.

From the beginning of her life, K felt that she was a disappointment and a trouble to her parents. I often ask people to tell me the story of their birth, and this is what K had to say:

'I gave mother a hard time. My parents say I was a disagreeable child—that I was always disagreeable. My mother was unconscious when I was born. She had had some gas. She didn't want any, but they gave it to her, and she was unconscious for a night and the next day. They had to take her to me—no, I mean me to her. She was too ill to come. Her having to go to me—no, me having to go to her, make me feel I wasn't wanted. My mother was sort of drowsy and couldn't take me. My dad saw me first. I don't know if he held me. The nurses had to coax her. They said: "Here's your baby. Take her."'

In my opinion, it was not so much that her mother didn't want her, but more the case that her mother had been simply unwell and 'lost' during a crucial moment. As an adult and a mother herself, relating what had happened according to what she had been told, as well as the feelings she had had, what becomes apparent from all this is a fundamental confusion concerning who is the mother and who is the child.

K's father had intended to go out for a big drinking session with his friends when K was born. However, when he found he had a daughter instead of a son he settled for a small get-together. K commented: 'Dad always wanted a boy, but when my brother came along he didn't help Dad like I did. I always tried to help him and please him, to show him that girls could do things.' She felt unrewarded for the trouble she took to please others. Her father had a small business in his country of origin and, on coming to the UK, had suffered a drop in status. Instead of employing people he had become a labourer. This had been hard for him to bear.

K was looked after by her mother for a few months, until she resumed full-time work, and then K was child-minded. When K was seven-years-old her elder sister joined the family, and the next year her brother was born. The family was now complete. Her mother gave up full-time work and stayed at home to take care of her son during the day, working part-time after K finished school. Her mother would leave the elder sister to care for K and her baby brother until father returned home.

K hardly saw her mother, and missed her deeply. She resented the changes she had to cope with, and envied the mothers she saw on television who spoke with and listened to their children. K longed for a mother who had the time and patience to listen, and who might treat her with respect.

However, K did enjoy school; it was a relief from her responsibilities at home. She had many jobs to do around the house, and hated the school holidays. When these arrived, in contrast to her peers, she would think to herself 'Oh my God: it's full-time for me now'. The 'holidays' consisted of full-time chores, and caring for her brother whilst the rest of the family went to work. She tried to please her parents by labouring at the housework, cooking, and minding her brother, but these were mostly carried out in a spirit of resentment. She felt largely unsuccessful in her efforts to please, and remarked: 'I've always jumbled things up'. This had become a trait of hers because, she believed, she had always tried to break her mother's rule that you should never wash and iron on the same day. She had had to break this rule simply in order to create more time for housework. K told me how she had never learnt to stop putting pressure on herself, because it was so important for her to feel admired within the family as 'a good little mother'. When she finally entered the adult world of work, she took this frame of mind along with her.

K felt keenly the absence of any tenderness from her parents. For instance, her menstruation was often painful, but she was told to keep busy, and 'not to treat periods as an illness'. She was expected to be out of bed and helping her mother, no matter how poorly she felt, and however much she felt like resting. Her mother was 'someone who never rested from morning until night'. Indeed, resting and relaxing in the course of a normal day was apparently not part of the family's routine; K informed me that her parents never relaxed, but simply went to sleep when they were tired. She craved more of their company, but felt pushed away from them.

K worried about under-achieving at school, yet was unable to accept help with her schoolwork from her family. She would struggle with it on her own, feeling unhelped and neglected. Her parents were pleased with her achievements, but she was not. She wanted more education—but even when she obtained it, in later life, she remained disappointed with herself.

As K approached adolescence her mother told her she was too argumentative, and that her constant questioning of everything made her mother ill. Family friends were asked to speak to K, and told her to behave herself, in order to prevent her mother from falling ill.

As an adolescent K wanted to take part in activities with her peers, but was prevented from doing so, because of her parents' fears that she might join with a bad crowd—and possibly also their fear that she might become pregnant, which would have been a re-run of her mother's life. Her parents' terror of anything beyond their immediate environment was taken in by K, and it stayed with her. For her, to stray beyond a pre-ordained boundary was to invite the occurrence of something terrible.

I think it is important not to underestimate just how anxious parents feel when it comes to the issue of the safety of their children. The information they give to the child is often accurate, but most often their methods of negotiating with the child are somewhat restricted. Their concern is of course based primarily on love. Even so, the wish for 'unquestioning obedience' may be rooted in anxieties which have their roots in the era of slavery. Whereas some families are able to raise children to think for themselves about their safety, the wish for total control which is encountered in other families can prove a great hindrance to psychological development. It was precisely this encouragement of the tendency to think for oneself which made Caribbean Independence movements possible in the first place.

From mid-adolescence onwards, K was aware of a growing anger towards her parents, which was kept in check mainly through fear of violence from her mother. She felt she was at war with her mother to a far greater extent than with her father. As she saw it she was utterly deprived of any status as a young adult, yet had been burdened with adult responsibilities since her childhood.

When she started work, and had met the first boyfriend who was 'not just interested in sex', she fell in love and married. She was twenty-years-old, and longing to escape from her parents' home. She had not considered living separately on her own as a realistic option, but had entered into marriage with a definite mission: 'to give my husband a sense of *ambition*'. In contrast to her own orderly, God-fearing, thrifty and hard-working family, her husband's relatives seemed somewhat spontaneous, disorderly, and easy-going. They did not appear to save money, or to make plans for the future. K's husband had a white mother and a black father, and had been brought up by his mother and the white man she subsequently married. In effect, he grew up in a white family. K wanted her husband and herself to save for and buy a house of their own, and they managed to do this very quickly. As she put it: 'we were continuing in the style of my parents' marriage'—which her husband admired.

K felt she had received good things from her parents, but that these had been spoilt by the way her parents had treated her. She felt she had been bullied, humiliated, restricted, intruded upon, prevented from having her own thoughts and feelings, and from showing her vulnerability. She commented: 'I'm as strong as my Mum. She could cope. She hid her feelings. But I can't hide my feelings like that. I'm not her—I'm me'.

What started out as a wish to be heard—to have her mother accept her separateness and difference—somehow developed into conflict between K and her mother. When father was at home he would usually intervene and put an end to their quarrelling. Even so, being repeatedly confronted drove K's mother 'mad' and, on one occasion, her mother attacked her. K escaped into another room in the house, but was followed by her mother who eventually caught hold of her, sat on top of her, and pinned her to the floor. From this position her mother proceeded to beat her, and to shout at her never to argue again. K had been determined not to let herself be terrorised during this ordeal. Afterwards, however, she was convinced that her mother had damaged her internal sexual organs, and this caused her a lot of anxiety.

K—like Little S's mother, in chapter eight—longed for closeness to her mother's body as a substitute for feeling held in her mother's mind. The manner of her entrance into the world, and the disrupted care she had received in her early childhood, meant that at adolescence—usually a time for separation—she found herself instead physically pinned down by her mother, in what she seems to have experienced as a kind of sexual assault.

K's experience of a bullying mother certainly influenced her choice of a husband. She made sure that if the bullying was going to continue then she would not be at the receiving end, as she had been in her childhood. She also ensured that her competence would be recognised by her husband, in a way which—she felt—it hadn't by her parents. From the outset she felt powerful in her marriage to this 'quiet' man. However, when her husband did assert himself, she found she could not share power with him; to K, power could be possessed by only one partner. When she sensed a loss of power to her husband she became intensely anxious.

* * *

K took her grievances over not being recognised as an adult into her place of work. In her job, her behaviour reminded me of Boxer, the horse, in George Orwell's *Animal Farm*:

Boxer was the admiration of everybody. He had been a hard worker even in Jones' time, but now he seemed more like three horses than one: there were days when the entire work of the farm seemed to rest upon his mighty shoulders. (Orwell 1954: 26)

This brought her into conflict with her female boss, onto whom K then transferred the uncomfortable feelings she had experienced as a child towards her mother. To be treated as a child was, for K, a humiliation. In her adult life she continued to expect such treatment and, as a result, experienced difficulties in negotiating her needs with other people. She was terrified of having her requests refused, which would have made her furiously angry. Consequently she was stuck in the position of trying to please her employers, just as she had struggled to please her parents. Her efforts to achieve were based not on the firm foundations of wanting to feel good about her self and to satisfy her own needs, but in order to demonstrate to others that she was good-enough after all. She was constantly striving to appease a tyrannical internalised parent, who was much more severe than her actual parents, and whose demands could never be assuaged.

Her demands for recognition were made in a way which proved unhelpful. So great was her desire to progress professionally, and at the highest possible speed, that she could not wait for a suitable vacancy to arise. Instead she demanded to be given more 'grown up' work, to which her boss responded by providing her with tasks suitable for someone of a higher grade, but without the salary to match. K accepted this, performed the work well, and gained valuable experience from it which she could have used to move on to a better job. Instead, however, she became locked in a furious battle with her boss. She claimed that her boss was discriminating against her on racial grounds, whereas in fact it was K who was responsible for placing herself in an exploited position. She kept herself so busy with the new responsibilities she had foisted upon herself that, when the opportunity did arise for a position at the higher grade she wanted, she allowed herself very little time to prepare her application. To me, her application seemed only a token gesture, a means of protecting herself from disappointment and the fear of failure, and also from the anxiety of actually getting the job and having to move up into the adult world she believed she craved. Unconsciously, she did not want the new position; her 'internal saboteur' seemed to be gaining the upper hand.

Her lack of confidence expressed itself in another incident: she applied for a job at a higher grade, but which she knew to be temporary. She believed that she would not be accepted within the organisation on any other basis, although there was no evidence for this, and her employers had demonstrated themselves willing to employ black people at a senior level. What might have seemed, on the surface, like an external problem of racial discrimination, on closer examination proved to be much more complex. K was deeply engaged in a course of action which was ultimately self-destructive. Her energy was becoming increasingly wasted on the struggle between parts of herself, preventing her from moving onwards when it was appropriate for her to do so. Instead she was repeating, in a compulsive way, behaviour that was no longer helpful to her.

People caught in this type of internal conflict often speak of feeling 'wasted', or of being 'given responsibility yet without any rewards'. They often become very depressed because they are full of unexpressed anger, which sometimes causes physical symptoms of bodily pain and high blood pressure. People who are otherwise able and talented, but who act out their feelings of abuse in the workplace, sometimes destructively recycle their frustration into their families, and may allow it seriously to undermine their health. In K's case, however, as her therapy continued she learnt to take rests, and to stand back from her attempts to control her husband's involvement with the children in their growing family. As a consequence, her relationships with all the family members improved.

Had she not received some help in thinking about what was happening both inside and outside herself, and about the connection between the two, then she might have continued to damage her prospects and those of her children. With her son J,

K merely went through the motions of reading to him; it was not done with any enjoyment. She read to him because she felt that that was what she was supposed to do, if she wanted him to do well at school. As a small child, K had not experienced for herself the pleasure of being read to. The lively Caribbean tradition of oral storytelling had been lost in her parents' transition to a new culture. For K there was no sense of excitement and discovery through verbal interaction, or through making up pictures in her own mind. Instead, pictures came from the television.

At the beginning of her therapy K informed me that it had been suggested she might have a hysterectomy to cure her abdominal pains. Clearly, surgery is necessary in cases of obvious malignant disease, but it seems to me likely that pain—even loss of blood from the uterus—calls out for a psychological as well as a medical investigation. K's abdominal pains caused me to consider the regularity with which women undergo hysterectomies, and what these operations might—in a psychical sense—be an attempt to cure. Had she not been in therapy, it seems to me very likely that K would have had her uterus removed in an attempt to alleviate pain that was centred in her mind rather than her body.

Despite K's experience of her upbringing, her parents brought many good things with them from the Caribbean. Unfortunately, however, it seemed they were unable to amalgamate the best of what they brought with the best of what they found in the UK. They became preoccupied with the dangers of the world beyond their home, from which the children had to be protected, and which the children could not be trusted to face on their own. Although dangers do sometimes exist in communities in which people live, this was not the case with K's family. Much of her parents' fear was unjustified, but of course this did not prevent K from internalising their anxiety. Indeed, even as an adult, the prospect of a journey across town would throw this competent, grown woman into a panic. Significantly, the only place she felt able to visit for a holiday was her parents' place of birth.

Those children of Caribbean parents who are the first to be born in the UK (as well as those of parents from other countries) are often expected to carry forward the hopes of the family for a better life. This can prove extremely burdensome in environments where these expectations are thwarted. The parents have often left behind their own parents and other relatives, which feeds the hope that the children might fill in the missing gaps. The children who are born in the new country can therefore arouse extreme emotional turmoil and upset in their parents, who are required to bestow the necessary care on their children yet without the nurturance of their own families, who have been left behind.

Ultimately, both K and her son J were able to obtain the individual personal attention they needed, through their experiences of therapy. The cycle of difficulties passing from one generation to the next was broken. The whole family benefited as a result of the therapeutic intervention, and found themselves in a much stronger position from which to deal with the outside world.

Chapter Twelve

When a Mother Dies

Seeds of rivalry and of open conflict between Caribbean Africans and migrants from India were sown in the period immediately following the abolition of slavery. After slavery, free men had the opportunity—for the first time—of organising their labour in order to receive the highest price for it. In response to this, however, the plantation owners simply imported indentured labour from India, China, Europe, and the region referred to today as the Middle East.

George Lamming, in his Foreword to Walter Rodney's *A History of the Guyanese Working People 1881-1905*, writes:

> Indentured labour was bound labour. It was deprived of all mobility and was therefore condemned to provide that reliability of service a crop like sugar demanded. The planter class, with the full permission of metropolitan power, had given itself the legal right to deploy this labour as it pleased... [W]hat the ruling class could not acquire by the normal play of the market forces had now been appropriated through legal sanctions. Indentured Indian labour was enslaved by the tyranny of the law that decided their relations to the land where they walked, and worked, and slept... The presence of this indentured labour had a direct and immediate effect on the bargaining power of the free labour force. (Lamming, in Rodney 1981)

As long as East Indians were prepared to undercut the wages of Africans, therefore, the wages of the Africans were kept low. For this reason, then, government policy sought to ensure the continuation of the indenture system.

Some of the indentured Indians understood clearly the manner in which they were being used, and therefore allied themselves with the Caribbean Africans. The Indians also had their own trade unions, which were engaged in struggles with the white bosses. Consequently, many Indians were convicted of breaches of labour contract. Evidently, then, in addition to the rivalry and conflict there were also attempts at co-operation between the races.

Indenture—like slavery—broke the connection between labourers and their families and their native language. The new arrivals, after abolition, were not beaten into giving up their language—as the African slaves had been. Instead their native languages fell into disuse over time, due to the necessity to communicate in Creole with those around them. They did, however, maintain their religion and culture, and eventually acquired land, and began to focus on making money in order to improve their social and economic status under the colonial government.

Unlike the Caribbean-based Africans, the Indian indentured labourers had voluntarily left their country, and so there was the possibility of returning home. Very few took up this opportunity, however, on account of the expense involved and the poverty they had sought to escape in the first place. Indenture was, in theory, only for a fixed period of time, and the money they earned—no matter how small the amount—was theirs to keep.

The African slaves had departed Africa after being hunted down by their own people and delivered into the hands of slavers. They were then forced to work the land without wages, under a rigidly organised and exceptionally cruel regime. This profoundly affected the attitude of the Caribbean Africans towards the land. The last thing they wanted to do was to work upon it—unless it belonged to them or they were able to acquire it (cf. Hart 1998: 40-44). Slavery also extinguished any thoughts of returning to Africa. They did not want to return to a land from which they had been forcibly removed by being sold as goods. It was not until the twentieth century that recovery from the trauma began—most notably due to the influence of Marcus Garvey in the 1920s. This displayed itself in what became a recognisable black consciousness movement. In the 1960s its forceful influence began to take effect in the Caribbean, the Americas, the UK, and in Africa itself.

For Indians—as well as for Africans in the Caribbean—English is the official spoken and written language. Creole, however, is either spoken or understood by all social groups. In Guyana and Trinidad, people of African and East Indian origin are well acquainted with one another's customs. They have also succeeded to a large extent in allowing one another to live in peace. However, in both these countries the African population has been overtaken in size by the Indian population. Both ethnic groups have migrated in substantial numbers to the UK and USA, where Indo-Caribbeans tend to demonstrate a reluctance to own up to their Caribbean heritage.

* * *

G, in her late thirties, came for psychotherapy as a consequence of problems she experienced at work. Professionally, she felt a failure. She also felt unable to make any decisions about her future.

In this chapter I am shifting the focus slightly, onto the people who arrived in the Caribbean after slavery was abolished, because G came from an Indo-Caribbean background. Her family were the descendants of people who had travelled from India to the Caribbean as indentured labourers after slavery was abolished.

According to East Indian tradition, G's mother lived with her in-laws after she married. It was a large family. However, a sibling, born after G, died during infancy, and this event had a great effect on her childhood. Equally decisive was her mother's decision—when G was under twelve months—to leave her in the care of a sister only eight-years-old, in order to join her husband working on the land. G believed that her paternal grandmother did not like her parents' side of the family, and that she preferred another daughter-in-law who also had a job away from home. According to G, the children of this woman received the most attention from their grandmother. G also suspected that it was the neglect of her grandmother which—later—caused her baby sibling to die. The older sister who helped care for G also died, when G reached the age of twelve.

G was aware of her mother being always over-tired and not much fun to be with. Her father, on the other hand, she described as light-hearted, and a very kind and open person. However, her father openly kept a mistress during G's childhood and adolescence, which resulted in serious financial hardship for the family. Although angry at her father for this, she was also grateful for the way he opened up to her the world beyond their small rural village. For instance, he frequently brought home foods for the family which originated from outside the Indian community.

G was a bright child, and won a scholarship to attend a secondary school away from the village. She performed well at school, whilst growing progressively aware of her family's social and economic position. She resolved to complete her education in order to help her family financially. In particular, she wanted to provide a better life for her mother, even though she was angry with her mother for—as she saw it—loving her father too much. G regarded living and working abroad as the only means of achieving her aims. Essentially, then, she saw herself as a rival to her father, and was determined to become a better provider than he had been. On leaving school she made serious plans to emigrate. Her father's death, and the subsequent attempt of an employer to rape her, speeded up the process of leaving.

* * *

G's arrival in the UK was a terrible shock to her system. She was unprepared for the cold climate, and soon became physically unwell. In the years that followed, she often responded to feelings of unhappiness by developing physical symptoms. The worst illness from which she suffered was a back complaint. She married a man whom she knew only slightly, but whom she had recognised as feeling just as deprived as herself. The marriage broke up within two years, after he was unfaithful to her. She suffered from backache constantly throughout her marriage.

After her divorce she took up further education, and then embarked on the career in which she found herself ten years later, at the start of her therapy. She felt at a complete standstill in her work. Although she was better educated and qualified than her mainly white bosses, she seemed convinced she did not have the qualifications necessary to obtain a better job. More recently, however, she had begun to tell herself that maybe she *did* have good qualifications, but it was her 'presentation' which was at fault. She made some perfunctory attempts at securing another job but soon gave up, and settled resentfully into a role well beneath her abilities. Her junior colleagues, meanwhile, regarded her as an expert in her field. They often sought her out for advice—a role which, she felt, awarded her some status but no responsibility, and no financial remuneration. She was locked in a rivalrous relationship with her boss, in much the same way she had been with her father, without any prospect of becoming a boss herself.

G's mother had died three years before she came to see me. G had travelled home for the funeral and, whilst here, had become extremely angry. She had accused her sister-in-law of not caring sufficiently for her mother, and they had almost come to blows. To G's great disappointment, her brother took his wife's side. She returned home to the UK deeply distressed, with no-one to help her mourn.

G attempted to deal with her grief by embarking on an extended, unpaid holiday. She journeyed to India, and then back to the Caribbean. Whilst she travelled, she often saw women of the same size and stature as her mother. She would overtake them in the street and then turn around to look at them. When she could see that they were not her mother, but total strangers, she felt dismayed and upset.

People spoke to her in India, presuming she could understand their language. She remembered smatterings of Hindi she had learnt from the hated grandmother, and she communicated as best she could, yet all the time she experienced a terrible emptiness and a profound sense of loss. She could not accept that her mother had died, and expected somehow to find her alive in India—the family's spiritual home. Travelling on, afterwards, to the Caribbean did not provide her with much comfort either. Since her mother's death the place seemed different; it no longer felt like home. Her siblings were now all grown up, and she did not feel needed.

G was troubled most of all by the loss of the sense of purpose which had brought her to the UK, and by the sheer reality of the traumatic changes which she had been unable to control. She wept with sorrow and guilt when she recalled the way in which she had not been there to care for her mother when she was ill and dying. She also wept for the part of herself which was still a small child, whose mother had not been there when *she* had needed her. She also recalled how devastated she had felt when her older sister had died. In G's mind her sister had been very much older than the eight years which separated them. She wept also for her father.

The loss of her mother put G in touch not only with the previous losses of her sister and her father, but also with the loss of her marriage and the possibility of a family of her own. For instance, during her divorce she saw her father standing at the top of a flight of stairs. She was concerned about telling anyone she had 'seen' her dead father, because she feared they would think she was mad. The experience did not frighten her; in fact, she felt that her father was remembering and comforting her with his 'visit'. Afterwards she told his ghost that he could now leave her. By doing this it seemed to me she was trying to hold on to her sanity, by accepting the reality of the separation. During her childhood and adolescence she had wanted to break up her parents by replacing her father. In the midst of the breakdown of her own marriage, then, she may have felt guilty and undeserving of a man of her own.

The loss of confidence she experienced in her working life came to a head when a professional decision, which she had made, had been overturned. Her anger was focused upon the person she held responsible for the humiliation she felt. This person was outside her immediate circle of colleagues. Internally, her colleagues represented her brothers and sisters. As with her siblings, she tried desperately to preserve her loving feelings towards them, but found herself entirely unable to go into work and be in the same room with them. The offending colleague, meanwhile, was Afro-Caribbean—that is, she was of a similar cultural background to G, but racially different. G felt thwarted and utterly dismayed by the way in which her boss had joined with this colleague in rejecting her decision. When this was subsequently upheld by a higher authority G was enraged.

The offending colleague seemed to stand both for G's sister-in-law (the one with whom she had almost come to blows), and her father's lover. Her father's unfaithfulness had blocked the resolution of G's Oedipus complex, by forcing her to take her mother's side. This, in turn, had made her relationships with men difficult. She desired her father, yet hated him because of his philandering. Her solution to the Oedipus complex had been to assume his place in relation to her mother, but—in this case —she was confronted with a subsequent dilemma of not possessing the penis with which she might satisfy her mother. Consequently, in her professional life, whenever she attempted to obtain something she wanted, she was overtaken instead by anxiety and forced to retreat. It was possible to understand how, when her mother died, G had begun to feel that everything was lost. It simply confirmed her suspicion that she 'did not have what it takes'.

G's expectation was that psychotherapy would make everything better within a month or two, and she was quite appalled at the prospect of a longer-term commitment. She was, however, able to see the connection between her angry feelings and her collapse, and this helped her return to work fairly soon. She also discovered a wish to explore her own mind a little more. She gained enough confidence to resume a relationship she had had with a man.

* * *

It was the question of who was the 'preferred sibling' which preoccupied G. Externally, in the dispute with her Afro-Caribbean colleague, her conflict was rooted in rivalries dating back to the post-slavery colonial period. Migration had transferred this rivalry from the Caribbean—in the same way it has transferred many other conflicts, from many other corners of the former British Empire, into the UK and North America.

At the same time, a quarrel was taking place in G's internal world: she was angry that she did not belong to the 'preferred family' (that is, to the favoured daughter-in-law's branch of the extended family); she was furious with her father for preferring his lover to either her mother or herself; and she was enraged at not being the 'preferred employee' at work. However, it is only when we view these disputes in their wider, socio-cultural and historical context, that we can understand the profound extent to which they are inter-connected.

Postscript

The sale of human beings inevitably takes its toll.

The families of Africans sold into slavery must have endured unimaginable fear and grief. It affected their well-being, and possibly the well-being of the whole African continent. The people sent away were never heard from again, and for those Africans made slaves in the plantations of the Caribbean, or in North and South America, a permanent severance of their connections with their families lay before them. Their past—their family name, history, and home—were systematically erased from history. It is a miracle that some sense of family history has nevertheless survived to the present day, by word of mouth, through songs, and through the efforts of linguists.

Even that which remained free—the possession of a mind of one's own; the enduring desire to form relationships—was nevertheless subject to heavy prohibitions. Attempts made by slaves to recover from their ordeal and maintain their humanity through loving relationships were interfered with and destroyed by the slavers. Planters and their employees physically and sexually abused men, women, and children. Relationships between slaves had to be kept absolutely secret, if the relationships were to survive, because to become a couple was one of the surest means of being sold off. Then, as now, it was thoroughly understood how potentially powerful a well-functioning family could be. Relationships between slaves, therefore, were broken in order to ensure better control of them by the planters who, although powerful themselves, lived in constant fear of rebellion.

The result of these events of long ago are conspicuous gaps in personal family histories. These gaps create problems for individuals, because they lead to feelings of not belonging, leading to discomfort and unhappiness. Any person whose family background has been influenced by slavery, and who knows something of the history of the slave trade, must chose for themselves whether to blame one side or the other (the buyers or the sellers) for what happened. What is important, however, is that Emancipation finally arrived. Yet it was not simply granted; it had to be fought for and died for by a few for the many. An awareness of the events leading to Emancipation fosters the hope that no matter how bad things may become they can be survived.

The legacy of fear passed on by the slave trade has disrupted the capacity of individuals for basic trust. It is well known how fundamentally important this basic trust is to the work of psychoanalysis. What I wish to stress, then, is that in our work with people affected by the legacy of slavery we must pay very careful attention to establishing and maintaining trust. As I hope to have shown, fear handed down through the generations plays a crucial part in the difficulties surrounding the resolution of the Oedipus complex. These difficulties are not simply the result of hatred. Fear itself puts the mind under severe pressure, placing it in a fragile state, in danger of disintegration.

Fear also finds expression in the vigilance which is necessary to prevent racial discrimination from growing worse. This vigilance can sometimes take on the form of suspicion, or the milder forms of paranoia. However, it would be wishful thinking to assert that this vigilance were no longer required in any form.

Despite the frequent, ritualised singing of 'Rule Britannia', with its line that 'Britons never, never, never shall be slaves', the teaching of children about the slave trade is utterly neglected in schools. The line in the song attests to the fear of a return of the aggressive attack made upon slaves. It seems to me, then, that the best form of vigilance against discrimination and violence grows from teaching children honestly about their history, and also from the parents of children to paying close attention to the feelings which arise in response to confronting history.

Racial discrimination continues to afflict us and to insinuate itself into peoples' lives. I hope to have made it clear that the internal world of each individual is complex. It is an interweaving of both external and internal reality, and the patient or client expects the psychoanalytic psychotherapist—or psychodynamic worker—to take on the full challenge of this complexity, in order that suffering might be understood and relieved. The difficulties of confronting feelings of fear, rage, depression, and lack of trust can be more easily worked with if the therapist begins to develop an understanding of the place from which the patient's feelings might be said to originate.

Bob Marley sang:

> Emancipate yourself from mental slavery.
> None but ourselves can free our minds! (Marley 1992)

I hope it will be remembered, then, that what is described in these pages concerns the lives of individuals, rather than a race of people.

Notes

[1] For instance, Hinsie and Campbell define fear as: 'a reaction to a real or threatened danger, while anxiety is more typically a reaction to an unreal or imagined danger' (Hinsie & Campbell 1975: 49).

[2] I refer the reader to the following sources for the historical material included in this chapter and throughout the book: Best 1979; Bush 1990; Estaban & Hennessy 1993; Fryer 1984; Gerzina 1995; Hart 1998; McFarlane 1977; Rodney 1972, 1981; Selvon 1998; Smith 1962; and Williams 1964.

[3] This is with the exception of Guyana and Trinidad where, in the 1990s, the East Indian population became the most numerous ethnic group.

[4] I imagine there were also Islamic Arabs who wished to see an end to slavery, but I am not acquainted with any written work on this subject.

[5] 'The Last of England' is in the Birmingham Art Gallery, and 'The Emigrant's Last Sight of Home' is in the Tate Gallery, London.

[6] Significant studies in this respect include Rosenfeld 1949, White 1961, Hermann 1980, Klein 1930.

[7] For an account of the development of Freud's thinking on neurosis, see the editor's introduction to *Inhibitions, Symptoms and Anxiety* (Freud 1926: 77-86), and the whole of this study itself.

[8] For a fuller account of Lacan's argument on psychosis, see Lacan 1993.

[9] See Lacan 1977, and also Laplanche & Pontalis 1988: 210, 439-41, for more detailed discussions of the imaginary and the symbolic orders.

[10] For a more detailed account of 'foreclosure' see Laplanche & Pontalis 1988: 166-169.

[11] Page numbers in brackets, given in the text of this and the following chapter, refer to the edition of Roy Heath's *The Murderer* published by Picador (London) in 1999.

[12] Winnicott uses the term 'maternally preoccupied' to describe an unfocussed state into which a mother enters, enabling her to become extremely sensitive to her infant's needs. He writes: 'I do not believe that it is possible to understand the functioning of the mother at the very beginning of the infant's life without seeing that she must be able to reach this state of heightened sensitivity, almost an illness and to recover from it. (I bring the word 'illness' because a woman must be healthy in order both to develop this state and to recover from it as the infant releases her. If the infant should die the mother's state suddenly shows up as illness. The mother takes this risk)' (Winnicott 1956: 302).

[13] An extended version of this chapter was published in *The British Journal of Psychotherapy* (Fletchman Smith 1993).

[14] To readers interested in the history of the black presence in the UK, I recommend Peter Fryer's *Staying Power* (1984).

[15] I have in mind the work of Caribbean male writers such as Roy Heath (1984, 1999) and Michael Thelwell (1980), and American women writers Maya Angelou (1969), Toni Morrison (1970), Alice Walker (1983), and many more besides.

[16] My observations here concern only a particular individual. It would, of course, be far too simplistic to claim that educational failure with regard to black boys can

be based entirely upon these causes, and I would not like it to be supposed I am arguing this. To me, an issue of far greater importance is the extent to which schools provide an environment free of fear as a means of safeguarding against educational under-achievement. An atmosphere in which hatred and ritual humiliation of boys is tolerated—arising out of fear—will not encourage the full development of potential, whether this occurs at school or at home.

17 'Permanency movement' is my term for a policy towards child-care which first appeared during the early 1980s, coinciding with the rise of Thatcherism (Fletchman Smith 1984). It prioritised the adoption of children in care, and emphasised the permanent severance of ties between the child and his or her natural family. This policy soon assumed precedence over: (a) the fostering of children with maintenance of ties with the natural family; and (b) long-term casework undertaken by social workers in conjunction with the natural family. The policy was first implemented in Scotland (Lothian), and was then taken up by Lambeth and Wandsworth Social Services Departments. It then spread to other local authorities and came to be regarded as 'best practice'. The policy came about as an over-reaction to the exposure of poor child-care provision in Rowe and Lambert's famous study *Children Who Wait* (1973).

Bibliography

Abraham, K. (1949) 'The Psycho-Sexual Differences Between Hysteria and Dementia Praecox', in *Selected Papers of Karl Abraham*, trans. D. Bryan & A. Strachey, London: Hogarth Press.

Angelou, M. (1969) *I Know Why the Caged Bird Sings*, London: Random House.

Angelou, M. (1998) *Even the Stars Look Lonesome*, London: Virago.

Bak, R. (1971) 'Object-relationships in schizophrenia and perversion', *International Journal of Psycho-Analysis* 52: 235-242.

Baumeyer, F. (1956) 'The Schreber case', *International Journal of Psycho-Analysis* 37: 61-74.

Best, G. (1979) *Mid-Victorian Britain 1851-75*, London: Fontana.

Bion, W.R. (1959) 'Attacks on Linking', in Bion 1967.

Bion, W.R. (1967) *Second Thoughts: Selected Papers on Psychoanalysis*, London: Maresfield Reprints.

Breuer, J., & Freud, S. (1893-5) *Studies on Hysteria*, S.E. II.

Brown, S., ed. (1984) *Caribbean Poetry Now*, London: Hodder & Stoughton.

Burke, A. (1984) 'Racism and psychological disturbance among West Indians in Britain', *International Journal of Social Psychiatry*.

Bush, B. (1990) *Slave Women in Caribbean Society 1650-1838*, London: James Curvey.

D'Aguiar, F. (1995) *The Longest Memory*, London: Vintage.

Dickens, C. (1982) *Hard Times* [1853], Oxford: Oxford University Press.

Ellenberger, H. (1970) *The Discovery of the Unconscious*, New York: Basic Books.

Estaban, M., Barnet, M., & Hennessy, A., eds. (1993) *The Autobiography of a Runaway Slave*, London: Macmillan.

Fairbairn, W.R.D. (1940) 'Schizoid Factors in the Personality', in Fairbairn 1984.

Fairbairn, W.R.D. (1956) 'Considerations arising out of the Schreber case', *British Journal of Medical Psychology* 29: 113-127.

Fairbairn, W.R.D. (1984) *Psychoanalytic Studies of the Personality*, London: Routledge & Kegan Paul.

Fletchman Smith, B. (1984) 'Effects of race on adoption and fostering', *International Journal of Social Psychiatry* 30.

Fletchman Smith, B. (1993) 'Assessing the difficulties for British patients of Caribbean origin in being referred for psychoanalytic psychotherapy', *British Journal of Psychotherapy* 10, 1: 50-61.

Freud, S. (1909) 'Analysis of a Phobia in a Five-Year-Old Boy' ['Little Hans'], S.E. X: 1-149.

Freud, S. (1911) 'Psycho-Analytic Notes upon an Autobiographical Account of a Case of Paranoia (Dementia Paranoides)', S.E. XII: 1-82.

Freud, S. (1917) 'Mourning and Melancholia', S.E. XIV: 237-258.

Freud, S. (1924a) 'The Loss of Reality in Psychosis and Neurosis', S.E. XIX: 181-187.

Freud, S. (1924b) 'Neurosis and Psychosis', S.E. XIX: 147-153.

Freud, S. (1926) *Inhibitions, Symptoms and Anxiety*, S.E. XX: 75-175.

Freud, S. (1930) *Civilization and Its Discontents*, S.E. XXI: 57-145.

Fryer, P. (1984) *Staying Power: The History of Black People in Britain*, London: Pluto Press.

Gerzina, G. (1995) *Black London Life Before Emancipation*, New Jersey: Rutgers University Press.

Hart, R. (1998) *From Occupation to Independence: A Short History of the Peoples of the English-Speaking Caribbean Region*, London: Pluto Press.

Heath, R. (1984) *Genetha*, London: Fontana.

Heath, R. (1999) *The Murderer*, London: Picador.

Hermann, I. (1980) 'Some aspects of psychotic regression: a Schreber study', *The International Review of Psycho-Analysis* 7: 2-10.

Hinsie, L., & Campbell, R. (1975) *Psychiatric Dictionary*, 4th edition, Oxford: Oxford University Press.

Hyatt Williams, A. (1960) 'A psychoanalytic approach to the treatment of the murderer', *International Journal of Psycho-Analysis* 41: 532-539.

Institute of Race Relations (1999) 'Racism in Employment', http://www.homebeats.co.uk/resources/employ.htm.

Kernberg, O. (1967) 'Borderline personality organisation', *Journal of the American Psychoanalytic Association* 15: 641-685.

Klein, M. (1930) 'The Importance of Symbol Formation in the Development of the Ego', in Klein 1988a.

Klein, M. (1940) 'Mourning and Its Relation to Manic Depressive States', in Klein 1988a.

Klein, M. (1946) 'Notes on Some Schizoid Mechanisms', in Klein 1988b.

Klein, M. (1952) 'The Emotional Life of the Infant', in Klein 1988b.

Klein, M. (1988a) *Love, Guilt and Reparation and Other Works*, London: Virago.

Klein, M. (1988b) *Envy and Gratitude and Other Works*, London: Virago.

Knight, R.P. (1940) 'The relationship of latent homosexuality to the mechanism of paranoid delusions', *Bulletin Menninger Clinic* 4: 149-159.

Lacan, J. (1977) 'The function and field of speech and language in psychoanalysis', in *Écrits: a Selection*, trans. A. Sheridan, London: Tavistock.

Lacan, J. (1993) *The Seminar of Jacques Lacan: Book III—The Psychoses, 1955-1956*, ed. J.-A. Miller, trans. R. Grigg, New York: Norton.

Laplanche, J., & Pontalis, J.-B. (1988) *The Language of Psycho-Analysis*, trans. D. Nicholson-Smith, London: Karnac Books.

McDougall, J. (1989) *Theatres of the Body: a Psychoanalytic Approach to Psychosomatic Illness*, London: Free Association Books.

McFarlane, A. (1977) *Cudjoe The Maroon*, London: Allison & Busby.

Marley, R.N. (1992) 'Redemption Song', from *Songs of Freedom*, Island Records.

Masson, J., ed. (1985) *The Complete Letters of Sigmund Freud to Wilhelm Fliess 1887-1904*, Cambridge MA: Belknap Press of Harvard University.

Morrison, T. (1970) *The Bluest Eye*, New York: Pocket Books.

Morrison, T. (1988) *Beloved*, London: Picador.

Niederland, W. (1951) 'Three notes on the Schreber case', *Psychoanalytic Quarterly* 20: 579-591.

Niederland, W. (1959a) 'The "miracled up" world of Schreber's childhood', *The Psychoanalytic Study of the Child* 14: 383-413.

Niederland, W. (1959b) 'Schreber: father and son', *Psychoanalytic Quarterly* 28: 159-169.

Niederland, W. (1960) 'Schreber's father', *Journal of the American Psychoanalytic Association* 8: 492-499.

Niederland, W. (1963) 'Further data and memorabilia pertaining to the Schreber case' 44: 201-207.

Orwell, G. (1954) *Animal Farm*, Harmondsworth: Penguin.

Rickman, J. (1957) 'Theory of the Psychoses', in *Selected Contributions to Psychoanalysis*, London: Hogarth Press.

Rodney, W. (1972) *How Europe Underdeveloped Africa*, London: Bogle L'Overture Publishers.

Rodney, W. (1981) *A History of the Guyanese Working People 1881-1905*, London: Heinemann.

Rosenfeld, H. (1949) 'Remarks on the Relation of Male Homosexuality to Paranoia, Paranoid Anxiety and Narcissism', in Rosenfeld 1982.

Rosenfeld, H. (1963) 'Notes on the Psychopathology and the Psycho-Analytic Treatment of Schizophrenia', in Rosenfeld 1982.

Rosenfeld, H. (1965) 'Psychopathology of Schizophrenia', in Rosenfeld 1982.

Rosenfeld, H. (1982) *Psychotic States*, London: Maresfield Imprints / Karnac Books.

Rowe, J., & Lambert, L. (1973) *Children Who Wait*, London: BAAF (British Agency for Adoption and Fostering).

Rycroft, C. (1985) *Psychoanalysis and Beyond*, London: Chatto & Windus.

Schreber, D. (1955) *Memoirs of My Nervous Illness*, ed. and trans. I. Macalpine & R. Hunter, London: William Dawson & Sons.

Selvon, S. (1998) *The Lonely Londoners*, London: Longman Caribbean Writers.

Sharpe, E. (1950) 'The Technique of Psychoanalysis', in *Collected Papers on Psychoanalysis*, London: Hogarth Press & The Institute of Psycho-Analysis.

Smith, R.T. (1962) *British Guiana*, Oxford: Oxford University Press.

Spring, W. (1939) 'Observations on world destruction fantasies', *Psychoanalytic Quarterly* 8: 48-56.

Thelwell, M. (1980) *The Harder They Come*, London: Pluto Press.

Waelder, R. (1976) *Psychoanalysis: Observation, Theory, Application*, ed. S. Guttman, New York: International Universities Press.

Walker, A. (1983) *The Colour Purple*, London: The Women's Press.

White, R. (1961) 'The mother conflict in Schreber's psychosis', *International Journal of Psycho-Analysis* 42, 1-2: 55-73.

Williams, E. (1964) *Capitalism and Slavery*, London: André Deutsch.

Winnicott, D.W. (1952a) 'Anxiety Associated with Insecurity', in Winnicott 1982.

Winnicott, D. W. (1952b) 'Psychoses and Child Care', in Winnicott 1982.

Winnicott, D.W. (1956) 'Primary Maternal Preoccupation', in Winnicott 1982.

Winnicott, D.W. (1960) 'The Theory of the Parent-Infant Relationship', in Winnicott 1965.

Winnicott, D.W. (1962) 'Ego Integration in Child Development', in Winnicott 1965.

Winnicott, D.W. (1965) *The Maturational Processes and the Facilitating Environment*, London: Hogarth Press.

Winnicott, D.W. (1967) 'Mirror Role of Mother and Family in Child Development', in Winnicott 1974.

Winnicott, D.W. (1974) *Playing and Reality*, London: Pelican Books.

Winnicott, D.W. (1982) *Through Paediatrics to Psychoanalysis*, London: Hogarth Press & The Institute of Psychoanalysis.

Index